UNDER A SACRED SKY

Essays on the Practice

and

Philosophy of Astrology

UNDER

A

SACRED SKY

Essays on the Practice
and
Philosophy of Astrology

Ray Grasse

The Wessex Astrologer

Published in 2015 by
The Wessex Astrologer Ltd,
4A Woodside Road
Bournemouth
BH5 2AZ
www.wessexastrologer.com

© Ray Grasse 2015

Ray Grasse asserts the moral right to be recognised as the author of
this work.

Cover Design by Jonathan Taylor
Cover Art: "Star of the Hero" (1936, tempera on canvas), by Nicholas
Roerich. By kind permission of the Nicholas Roerich Museum,
New York.

A catalogue record for this book is available at The British Library

ISBN 9781910531075

for Laurence Hillman

Contents

Author's Preface

This book features a collection of my articles published over the last 20 years, exploring different facets of astrology and its symbolism. Broadly speaking, these fall into two primary categories: personal astrology – how the horoscope illuminates the lives and psychologies of individuals – and mundane astrology, which focuses more on historical trends and socio-cultural patterns. Since they first appeared in print, I've updated some of them to reflect my current thinking and research, and rewritten certain passages to avoid unnecessary repetition. With all of them, I've attempted to convey the ideas to as broad a segment of readership as possible so that both beginners and advanced students of astrology might gain some insight from the themes presented. I hope you, the reader, find it valuable.

Ray Grasse
Chicago, July 2015

1

The Enchanted Cosmos:
Symbolism, Synchronicity, and the
Astrological World View

The universe is composed of stories, not atoms.
Muriel Rukeyser, *The Speed of Darkness*

I recently met with a client whose natal horoscope included an especially volatile Mars positioned exactly on his 4th-house cusp – the segment of the horoscope relating to home and domesticity. During the course of our conversation, the young man told me of a curious event that occurred at the moment he was born: exactly as his mother was at the hospital giving birth to him, a small fire broke out back at the family home, causing extensive damage to one of several bedrooms.

A curious synchronicity, I thought, considering the "fiery" pattern in his chart relating to the home – and considering the ongoing pattern of domestic turbulence this individual experienced throughout his life ever since.

Over the years of researching various aspects of symbolism and synchronicity, I've encountered many such stories, not only from discussions with clients but from a variety of historical sources as well. In many Native American cultures, for example, it's well known that special attention was paid to signs or symbols occurring in the environment at the moment of a child's birth. So if a child was born at the moment a deer happened to run by, that *that* child might be named Running Deer, in the belief that personality would grow up to express qualities of swiftness or gracefulness.

Or, in the Tibetan tradition, if a great earthquake occurred at the moment of a child's birth, this might be taken as a sign this individual would somehow have a great or unusual destiny, and might likewise "shake the world." Western classical history tells us of similar symbols or omens that accompanied the births of figures like Alexander the Great, Socrates, and Plato. Indeed, there are few traditional cultures which did not place emphasis on such symbols or "coincidences" around the births of men and women.

As with astrology, signs like this have traditionally been thought to reflect the destinies or characters of the individuals involved – with or without added consideration of the celestial configurations of the moment. Applying this approach to my own client's case, any esotericist worth their salt would have immediately recognized an important insight into this person's life simply from observing the symbols in the environment around his birth – in this case, "Martian" symbols.

Simply put, while the starry sky offers a profound map into the soul and destiny of an individual, it is by no means the only map available within the symbolic landscape of our environment.

Examples like this open a window into an important but often overlooked dimension of astrology, and invite us to reconsider a very old question: *How does astrology work*? If there is indeed a vital connection between the celestial bodies and our lives down here on Earth, what specifically is the *mechanism* involved?

Over the millennia, any number of theories have been put forth to explain astrology's inner workings, most of which can, in simplest terms, be classified into one of two primary groups: *causal*, or force, explanations, and *acausal*, or synchronistic, explanations.

According to the *causal* model, humans are influenced by means of an energy or force transmitted from celestial bodies to creatures down on Earth. For some writers, that's to be explained in terms of an already known force like electromagnetism or gravity. Astrophysicist Percy Seymour, for example, writes about the complex way the Solar System interacts with the Earth's geomagnetic fields:

> The whole solar system is playing a symphony on the magnetic field of the Earth... We are all genetically 'tuned' to receiving a different set of melodies from the symphony.[1]

For still others, this causal force consists of an energy within nature that's still to be discovered by science – and might even be para- normal or occult in nature, as was believed by Rennaissance magical philosophers like Cornelius Agrippa. In either case, such "force" theories hold that celestial forces act upon humans by means of a classical cause-and-effect mechanism; in short, this affects that.

On the other hand, the *acausal* or synchronistic explanation believes that the secret of astrological influence won't ever be found in any purely mechanistic theories of cause-and-effect, but only in conjunction with a more holistic worldview that views all phenomena as embedded in a deeper network of interconnectedness and meaning. According to writers like Dane Rudhyar and H.P. Blavatsky, the planetary patterns at one's moment of birth don't *cause* particular traits or tendencies so much as *reflect* them. The simultaneity of celestial and earthly events are, to use Carl Jung's terminology, a "meaningful coincidence," with the position of the planets and the life of individual's lives representing joint expressions of the same underlying pattern of meaningfulness.

In this essay, we will look more closely at the idea that astrology is indeed synchronistic – but with a twist. The "mechanism" of astrology could be more accurately described as *symbolism*, whereby celestial events not only connect acausally with earthly happenings but also incorporate dimensions of symbolism and meaning beyond their surface appearances. As evidence for this point, consider the fact that of all the myriad techniques and theories employed by astrologers, the vast majority of these are entirely symbolic in character, with little or no basis in empirical, concrete reality. Here are just a few examples:

- The complex network of hidden correspondences believed by astrologers to link the diverse areas of our lives, in ways that are profoundly metaphorical and archetypal in nature.

- The otherwise perplexing division of both houses and zodiacs specifically into twelve segments, suggesting an archetypal rather than practical basis. (Why not eight? Six? Or, more logically, four?).

- The method of classic progressions, based on a day-for-a-year movement of the planets from their position at one's time of birth.

- The art of horary astrology, whereby horoscopes are cast for such seemingly intangible things as questions or even ideas.

- Astrology's employment of planets positioned below the horizon in casting horoscopes. In any purely force-based model, subtle influences like this (all the more minimized in the case of distant planets like Pluto or Neptune) would logically seem blocked by the sheer mass of the Earth; in the symbolic model, though, such factors simply assume more hidden dimensions of meaning.

- The vast array of abstract points and "parts" employed in Arabic, Vedic, and some Western schools of astrology, arrived at through purely mathematical or symbolic, rather than observational, means.

- The mysterious manner whereby horoscopes appear to operate even after their owners' deaths. For instance, mythological scholar Joseph Campbell achieved his greatest fame posthumously, when a series of televised interviews with him by Bill Moyers appeared on public television shortly after his death – right at the point when Campbell would have been experiencing his Uranus return. In a simlar way, when Clint Eastwood's film about J. Edgar Hoover, *J. Edgar*, premiered in late 2011, it occurred just as transiting Pluto (the planet of resurrection) began crossing over Hoover's natal Sun-sign planets. If astrology is based on a causal "force" of some kind, how could it operate after the person is not even *alive* anymore?

As one final example of astrology's symbolist dimension, consider the widely-used concept of retrogradation. A planet like Mercury is said to be retrograde when its skyward path relative to the Earth seems to reverse itself. In actuality, of course, Mercury is traveling in its orbit around the Sun just as the Earth is. However, in much the same way that a train overtaken by a faster train might seem to be moving backward when in fact it's still moving forward along its own path at a steady rate of speed, the reversal of Mercury is a perceptual illusion caused by its position relative to the Earth's slower orbital path.

When Mercury's apparent motion reverses itself for several weeks at a time, business contracts begun then seem to develop complications, communications may stall, and technical difficulties arise. While most contemporary astrologers also allow for the possibility of positive effects accompanying these periods, these are generally seen as involving more psychological or spiritual levels of experience.

The effects of a Mercury retrograde are observable and borne out by personal experience; but the cause-and-effect, or force, model can't possibly account for them. Clearly, it's nonsensical to speculate about "backing up" rays or "retrograde emanations" coming from the planet itself, since the retrograde phenomenon has nothing to do with the objective status of Mercury. Rather, the celestial "reversal" of Mercury is better understood as a metaphor for conditions taking place for humans, existing only in relation to the phenomenological dynamics of observers on Earth.

Astrology, then, as the yogi and mystic Shelly Trimmer once suggested, is best defined as *astronomy, symbolically interpreted*. Said another way, astrology uses the same essential facts as astronomy but infuses them with a symbolic or qualitative dimension that's absent for the conventional scientists. As seen by astronomers, for example, Jupiter is simply a large gaseous planet with certain measurable properties, traveling at a particular speed, in a particular orbital path. For astrologers, however, Jupiter symbolizes a particular set of *qualities*: expansiveness, joviality, excess, exploration, spiritual learning.

Importantly, this astrological interpretation can't be grasped through strictly scientific, quantitative means. If one traveled to that distant planet and took samples of its gasses, or tried to measure its energy fields, one still wouldn't be able to isolate the symbolic meaning associated with the planet by astrologers. And that's because astrological interpretation requires a perceptual shift, a kind of metaphoric knowing.

But we need take this one vital step further. The worldview underlying astrology doesn't regard simply the planets but *all of reality* as symbolic and meaning-laden. To the symbolist, the heavenly bodies are only threads within a far greater tapestry of affinities. As Emerson wrote:

> Secret analogies tie together the remotest parts of Nature, as the atmosphere of a summer morning is filled with innumerable gossamer threads running in every direction, revealed by the beams of the rising sun![2]

Thus, when a child is born, the symbolist can find important clues pointing to the child's character and destiny everywhere – in the flight of birds, the movement of clouds, and other natural signs and omens; in coincidences and events in the lives of the parents and their community; in political and social happenings; as well as in the position of the stars and planets at the moment of birth.

The mystical Neoplatonic philosopher Plotinus, who is often misinterpreted as being critical of astrology, echoes this understanding. In *Ennead II.3*, his primary essay on this subject, Plotinus criticizes the *simplistic* understanding of astrology which holds that stars "cause" things to happen on Earth. Rather, Plotinus argues that astrological influence is based on a philosophy of cosmic unity. Since all things emanate from the One, or the Divine Source, all things are intricately coordinated or "enchained" with one another and are therefore "signifiers" of each other within a supremely regulated design – the stars no less so than birds or any other phenomena. Plotinus wrote, "The wise man is the man who in any one thing can read another."[3]

In other words, the stars and planets are meaningful, just as every other object or event is meaningful, since all things are equally intertwined within a grand universal order. As Plotinus remarks elsewhere, one would have to be far removed from the awareness of Divine Unity to think that anything is truly accidental or the result of chance.

Given this philosophical framework, questions of "mechanism" almost seem inappropriate. Does a Native shaman who names their child "Swift Eagle" because of the great bird circling the village during their birth, ask what manner of force emanated from the eagle towards the child, influencing its personality and destiny? Do they wonder by what means this force is transmitted, or its precise speed? More useful than such queries is an appreciation of the wonder of a universe in which such synchronicities occur, in which meaning expresses itself in manifold and multi-dimensional ways, not only through planets and people, but animals, weather, colors, landscapes – in short, every perceivable thing, both large and small. As Plotinus wrote:

> All things must be enchained, and the sympathy and correspondence obtaining in any one closely knit organism must exist, first, within the All.[4]

Even asking what influence the planets have on human beings conceals a fundamental misconception, since the planets themselves are only facets of a larger picture in which each element interlocks with the other in a mutually arising symphony of meaning.

One final analogy may help make this point clearer. Imagine a play where the lead character finally awakens to a truth he's long hidden from himself. As the playwright penned the scene, the moment of his break-through is accompanied by the image of a rising Sun depicted off at the back of the stage – a dramatic device meant to complement the change of heart experienced by the lead character.

Now, how should we understand the relationship between the sun-rise and the psychological change of character? Are there any secret "rays" emanating from the mock-Sun to the lead character which a sci-entist could measure and quantify? Is there some energy field set up amongst the characters acting on stage, or amongst the objects and props which comprise the backdrop? Clearly, there isn't. Nonetheless, there is a connection between the character's psychological shift and the lighting change – but it's a symbolic rather than causal one. Each element in the story unfolds within a larger framework of meaning and is interpretable only in relation to a transcendent, or "implicate" ground of reference – the dramatic design conceived in the mind of the playwright.

Here, as in astrology, meaning can only be accessed through the lens of symbolic understanding. Each person's experience represents a unique and highly personalized context of meaning. The seemingly un-related events of someone's life – which include, among other things, the positions of the stars and planets in the sky – are best understood as mu-tually arising elements in a greater field of significance, the archetypal script of a life and consciousness, as reflected in the horoscope.

The astrological worldview is, therefore, one in which each person's life is regarded as a living book of symbols, unlocked through the key of metaphoric knowing. Like a kind of "waking dream," each person's world is an archetypal drama containing multiple levels of resonance and interconnectedness, encoding information about the past, present, and future.

The astrological cosmos is indeed, using Muriel Rukeyser's won-derful phrase, a world of stories rather than atoms, better understood through the eye of the poet than the instrumentations of science. Like solar systems in stately procession around a vast galaxy, so all personal stories are nested within greater stories, broader contexts of meaning, each level providing a deeper and broader perspective on the meaning of that personal dream, the personal horoscope. Like Ezekiel's "wheels within wheels," the astrological cosmos is a vast web of ascending hier-archies, each increasingly objective vantage point yielding a more com-plex worldview, each one apt and true for that level. "A subtle chain of countless rings," wrote Emerson, "the next unto the farthest brings..."[5] Perhaps, as mystics have suggested, all personal dramas converge on an ultimate hub of meaningfulness, variously known as the Tao, Brahma, the Cosmic Dreamer, the Ground of Being, or, simply, the Absolute. At this still center point, perhaps, a great consciousness holds the enchanted cosmos in balance. As the German philosopher Schopenhauer expressed it over a century ago:

> It is a vast dream, dreamed by single being; but in such a way that all the dream characters dream too. Hence, everything interlocks and harmonizes with everything else.[6]

Notes

1. Percy Seymour, *Astrology: The Evidence of Science*. (Luton Beds, Eng-land: Lennard Publishing, 1988), p. 13.
2. Ralph Waldo Emerson, *The Complete Writings, Vol. II* (New York, Wil-liam H. Wise, 1929), p. 949.
3. Plotinus, *The Enneads*, translated by Thomas MacKenna. (Burdett, NY: Larson Publications, 1992) *Ennead II. 3.7*, pp. 108-109.
4. ibid, p. 109.
5. Ralph Waldo Emerson, "Nature," *The Complete Writings, Vol. II* (New York, William H. Wise, 1929), p. 913.
6. Arthur Schopenhauer, cited by Joseph Campbell, *The Masks of God, vol. IV: Creative Mythology*, (New York: Viking Press, 1968), p. 344.

Reprinted from *The Mountain Astrologer*, December/January 1997-98.

2

The Divine Science:
Reflections on a Life in Astrology

Every man is more than just himself; he also represents the unique, the very special and always significant and remarkable point at which the world's phenomena intersect, only once in this way, and never again.

Hermann Hesse, *Demian*

As I sat down on the floor across from the astrologer, I watched as she carefully studied the sheet of hieroglyphic-type symbols laid out before her. Her name was Debbie, a classmate from college. When she mentioned one day between classes that she did horoscopes on the side, I was fascinated enough to check this out for myself. My only experience with astrologers up to this point had been a casual conversation with a novice practitioner one year earlier, but that didn't go well at all. This would be my first formal reading from a real, working astrologer. I wasn't a believer nor a disbeliever at this point, but I'd heard just enough about the subject to think it might hold some value.

I can't say when or where I first heard about this subject, since it was in the air throughout my childhood. Besides the ubiquitous newspaper columns featuring Sun-sign astrology, it wasn't unusual in those days to turn on the radio and hear songs with lyrics like "When the Moon is in the 7th house and Jupiter aligns with Mars," or hear celebrities on talk shows refer to their horoscopes. A more serious turning point for me came in my mid teens when a friend handed me a book titled *Astrology* by Joseph Goodavage. It offered a useful overview of the topic and piqued my curiosity about the possibility that there really could be something to this subject after all.

But actually having someone do your horoscope was a different matter altogether from just reading books or hearing celebrities talk about it on the TV. This felt far more personal, and held out the promise of probing deeper into my life than the newspaper columns possibly could. So I was told. I was only 19 at the time, very unsure of myself, and more than a bit nervous about what Debbie might uncover. After all, the books almost made it sound as though astrology gave you a kind of X-ray vision into the very soul. Yikes.

The next hour or so, she proceeded to tell me things about my personality and life that were at once both astonishing and mysterious. Astonishing, because her reading was surprisingly accurate – like her comment about my probably having had abdominal surgery in early childhood; or her remark about a romantic disappointment I had experienced just a few weeks earlier.

Mysterious, because I wondered how it was possible for someone who didn't really know me to look at bizarre markings on a piece of paper like that and say things about my life she had no way of knowing – all extrapolated just from planetary positions in outer space. It was all unspeakably weird.

The Teachers
I went away from that session more curious than ever, but it was another two years before I began formal studies of the subject. My first instructor was Maura Cleary, a brilliant woman who'd previously spent several years at the University of Chicago teaching with such luminaries as Mircea Eliade, Eugene Gendlin, Paul Ricoeur, and James Hillman – all while still in her mid twenties. Specializing in the work of Carl Jung, she originally set out to disprove astrology, expecting this to be a relatively easy affair, with the intention of publishing her results in the popular new publication *Psychology Today*. But while studying under veteran Chicago astrologer Norman Ahrens (and, later, Pearl Marks), she soon discovered just how accurate – and profound – this discipline was, not to mention its deep relevance to the work of Carl Jung. I also found out that, prior to her stint at the university, she had spent time as a novice at a convent in Kentucky. In some ways, I was almost as interested in learning about her as I was in learning about astrology.

Her teachings opened my mind to a host of new ideas, including the concept that each of us is intimately connected to the workings of the universe. One day she made this thought-provoking comment:

Because each person is an embodiment of the universe at the moment they're born, if you were to take everyone on the planet and line them up according to birth order, you'd have a living portrait of the universe itself.

Astrology hints at powerful secrets, that was clear: Jupiter, the Sun, Mars, and the other planets aren't really outside of us; they're a part of us, and we are a part of them. In a sense, our true nature is as vast as the universe itself. I felt as though my mind was expanding by the day.

The late 1960s and early '70s were a magical and serendipitous time in many ways, when it seemed comparatively effortless to find exciting teachers or teachings of an esoteric bent. Another catalyzing figure for me in that regard was Goswami Kriyananda, a Chicago-born yogi and mystic (not to be confused with the California-based teacher of a similar name). Kriyananda wasn't as overtly psychological in approach to astrology as Maura, but his knowledge of the discipline was both encyclopedic and inspiring. During my nearly 15 years of study with him, he taught such diverse factors as methods of prediction, the intricacies of karma, esoteric astrology, the relation between the planets and the chakras, and an assortment of other concepts associated with this celestial science.

Over time, it became obvious to me that there was far more than simple book-learning behind Kriyananda's understanding of the subject. Consider the time a friend came with me to his center to hear him lecture, and sat near Kriyananda's podium as he delivered a talk to a small group of students. At one point, Kriyananda casually turned to my friend and mentioned, in passing, some of the planetary energies my friend was experiencing at the time. What made that so unusual was the fact that my friend had never divulged his birth information to Kriyananda or anyone else at the center, other than me. So surprised was my friend by Kriyananda's comments that he decided to head into his office after the lecture to ask how he knew what was going on in his horoscope. "I could see it in your spine," Kriyananda replied. To him, the horoscope was a reflection of the deeper energies inside one, or what the yogis called the chakras. If one were psychic enough, it seems, one could look into any person's spinal currents and glean a sense of what was unfolding in their horoscope. Experiences like that ignited a curiosity in me for that horoscope/chakric connection that I would pursue (and write about) for many years afterward.

From there, it was a logical jump to study with Kriyananda's own teacher, Shelly Trimmer (1917–1996), another yogi in the Kriya tradition. Part Kabbalist, part ceremonial magician, and part mystic, this man had studied for several years during the early 1940s with the famed Swami Paramahansa Yogananda. Shelly brought to his understanding of astrology a body of mystical insight and esoteric knowledge unlike anything I'd encountered before, or for that matter, since. He lived in Bradenton, Florida during the years we interacted, and taught primarily on a one-to-one basis, scrupulously shunning publicity in favor of a more personal-

11

ized approach to instruction. When I once asked him why he had never written any books, he answered simply, "My students are my books."

Whether he was talking about astrology, time travel, or quantum physics, I sometimes had the eerie sensation I was dealing with someone who'd just arrived from some point in the future. Among other things, Trimmer regarded astrology as a key to the mysteries of consciousness itself:

> The symbols around us are a reflection of our state of consciousness, and they can tell us a great deal about who we are and our relative level of spiritual awareness. If someone truly knows the laws of symbols, you could set that person down anywhere in the universe or on any plane of existence, and they'd be able to figure out where they are in the scheme of things. If you understand symbols, you'll always have a way of orienting yourself.

Like Yogananda, Trimmer emphasized the importance of knowing your horoscope but not becoming too bound by it. The horoscope is a map of karmic patterns and past-life memories, but he stressed that one's spiritual nature transcends the horoscope and its symbols. By learning to balance your energies in the center of the spine – the subtle channel that yogis refer to as *sushumna* – you can become free from the compelling forces of karma and transcend the influences of the horoscope. That doesn't mean that you no longer encounter problems in the outer world, simply that they don't exert the same influence on your awareness. He remarked:

> When your awareness is "on the wheel" [i.e., focused within the subtle currents to the right and left side of the spine], you'll always be "crucified," you'll be controlled by the forces of fear and desire, and by your horoscope. But when you learn to balance your energies within the proverbial "straight and narrow" [sushumna], you are free. Then you're able to work with the energies of the horoscope in a more constructive and creative way. Rather than the horoscope controlling you, you now control the horoscope.

Building a Practice

I continued to read voraciously on the subject, my interest stirred by writers like Charles Carter, Dane Rudhyar, Stephen Arroyo, Rob Hand,

and Alan Oken, among others, and I set about calculating the charts of everyone I knew. As a way to hone my skills, I started by offering free readings to people and, before long, began doing horoscope readings professionally. My clients eventually came to comprise a diverse group of individuals from all walks of life. Most were simply looking for guidance in matters of romance or career, but there were more unusual cases, too: rock musicians, writers and actors, a few New Age celebrities, a former lawyer for the Watergate trial, some politicians, stock market investors, and even a prostitute or two. Like I say, diverse.

I also spent a great deal of time studying the birth charts of the mega-famous, since their lives were open books and provided marvelous case histories for investigation. That led to some interesting encounters along the way, as I sought to track down exact birth times when they weren't publicly available. Occasionally, I'd find myself tongue-tied when actually crossing paths with these notable people, as happened with Aaron Copland, Frank Zappa, and Marshall McLuhan. But on other occasions, I mustered up the self-confidence to make contact, whether that was on the street, in an airport, or at some public event.

One of those celebrities was the author of the *Dune* books, Frank Herbert, with whom I spoke at length at a book-signing when no one else was around. During our conversation, he not only seemed sympathetic toward astrology but explained that his wife actually practiced astrology herself. On another occasion, I had the good fortune of speaking with futurist Buckminster Fuller, whose work and life I had long admired. I knew his birthday but not his moment of birth, and was eager to find that out. When I asked if he knew his exact birth time, he paused a while – leading me to wonder whether my question might have seemed foolish or even impertinent. Instead, a look of wistfulness came over his face, as he gave an answer that any astrologer would find intriguing: "I've always regretted not asking my mother that …"

Probably my most interesting encounter of all, though, was the time I called up science fiction writer Isaac Asimov in 1978. I knew he claimed to be skeptical about all things metaphysical (a smokescreen, I suspected, since he also professed to being deeply superstitious!), but I was fascinated by his books on science and his short stories like "Nightfall." So, when I read in an interview that his Manhattan phone number was listed publicly, I called up telephone enquiries in New York City and readily obtained it. Taking a deep breath, I dialed his number; it rang a few times, and – to my surprise – he answered it himself. That caught me off guard, since I expected he'd surely have a secretary or assistant answering his calls. After some hemming and hawing on my part, I told him I'd like to obtain his birth data for a project I was working on. (Coward that I was, I wasn't quite ready to tip my hand as to my true reasons for calling.) He told me that not only was he uncertain of his birth time, he wasn't even sure of his exact birth day, because he was born in Russia during an era when records were not well kept.

He didn't seem annoyed about being intruded upon like this – not at first, anyway – so I took the liberty of bringing up astrology, to get his opinion of it. I mentioned that I was studying the subject and was curious to see how his horoscope coincided with his life and personality. He was open to this, but countered with an intriguing suggestion: "How about if I gave you the details of someone's life, and you come up with their horoscope?" That was an idea I'd heard before from skeptics, and astrologers even have a term for this sort of thing: rectification. Unfortunately, I also knew that this was an especially difficult way to study astrology's workings, because although a person's horoscope is reflected in the circumstances of their life, the circumstances of their life could be the result of many different horoscopic combinations, not just one. I tried my best to explain that subtlety, but didn't do a very good job of it, and he eventually grew silent as I continued talking. I got the feeling this was his way of politely letting me know that I'd overstayed my welcome, so I took the hint, thanked him for his time, and said goodbye. It may just be a coincidence, but I learned shortly afterward that he removed his phone number from the Manhattan phone book.

Intimations of a Divine Order
Early on, I realized what a powerful tool the astrological system could be, for good or ill. At its best, I saw that I could use astrology to help clients better understand their latent strengths and weaknesses, and help them to see their lives more clearly. When it came to predictive readings, I could chart the ups and downs of the year ahead so they could best take advantage of those trends. I often used the analogy of someone going on a trip across the country: You might spontaneously decide to make your way along the roads and highways without any set itinerary, and that has

its own obvious appeal. But if you at least had a map, it would probably make the trip run more smoothly. A map allows you to get your bearings within the larger journey. In much the same way, the horoscope gives you a "road map" through time, and helps you to better understand the landscape of the changes that lie ahead on your life's journey.

At worst, I also saw how powerfully we astrologers can impact our clients' lives in problematic ways by what we say to them and how we say it. That's true for anyone working in a counseling profession, to be sure, but it seems to pose an even greater risk in the astrological trade because the client can view the information as coming from a quasi-Divine source – it is written in the stars. When I first began looking into astrology, I had my own unfortunate experiences with a few armchair astrologers, and knew full well how even a single negative comment could skewer someone's perspective for months, possibly even years. While I've made a few mistakes like that myself, from time to time, those early experiences made me especially conscious of how critical it is to frame one's information for clients in as constructive a fashion as possible.

The dimension of astrology that had the greatest impact on my way of thinking, however, was its philosophical implications. It's nearly impossible to practice this discipline for any length of time and not have your worldview shaken up in significant ways when you're confronted by instances so startling that you're led to stand back and wonder, "What on Earth is going on here?" For example, I'd look at someone's chart and see that Saturn had just crossed over their Ascendant, so I'd ask if they'd experienced any problems with their teeth lately (since Saturn rules the teeth) – only to be told that they had just undergone a root canal two days earlier. I'd wonder to myself: What does that Ringed Planet out there have to do with teeth? It was as though astrology hinted at a bizarre network of connections behind the scenes that made no sense from any ordinary standpoint and yet was borne out in reality time after time.

Once, I was studying a client's horoscope and realized that Neptune was going to affect her horoscope soon in a way that could possibly be dangerous. While quietly telling her about the emotional challenges this might pose, I also mentioned a few practical tips as well. Knowing that she lived by the ocean, I suggested that she consider avoiding boats or swimming in the ocean for the time being, since these are areas traditionally ruled by Neptune. When the predicted time rolled around, my client studiously avoided boats and bodies of water, just as I prescribed – but apparently those things weren't quite ready to avoid her. While she was driving down the highway one afternoon, an accident occurred in the oncoming lane, involving a car with a small boat hitched behind. The collision sent the now-unhitched boat through the air at a high speed; it careened over her own car and missed her by just inches.

Here again, this begs the question: What possible connection could a planet way out there have to do with earthbound objects like boats? It seemed absurd, yet I couldn't deny the reality of such synchronicities. Examples like this suggested, among other things, that astrology is above all a language of symbols and that reality itself is written in the language of symbols. Our world isn't simply a mass of dead matter, in other words, but is suffused with meaning. In that spirit, I came to see our universe as being more akin to a great mythic novel than a dry science textbook.

In cases like that of my Neptunian client, I also saw that astrology pointed toward something equally profound – namely, the presence of a transcendent intelligence choreographing all events down to the finest detail. How else could one explain the way different lives intertwined so perfectly in a situation like my client experienced with the boat? If she had happened to arrive at that point in the highway just ten minutes earlier, she would have missed the accident altogether. So, what brought those different lives together so perfectly, right when the planets in her horoscope lined up in a symbolically complementary way, like interlocking parts of a cosmic Swiss watch? This wasn't hard proof of the existence of a God, I realized, but it surely hinted at some regulating intelligence at work throughout the universe, whatever name one preferred to call it.

In a more modest but no less important way, astrology also expresses the incredible uniqueness of each individual's life. Each of us is the center of our own universe, since there is no one else who shares our unique perspective. I often found myself reminded of that passage from Hermann Hesse I'd read years earlier (which opens this essay), suggesting that we are not "just ourselves," but rather a remarkable and unique intersection of all the world's phenomena, a singular expression of our universe. To this day, every person's chart I look at offers me a reminder of that awe-inspiring fact.

Reprinted from *The Mountain Astrologer*, October/November 2012.

3

Saturn, the Late Bloomer:
Understanding the Long-Range Dynamics of Saturn in the Horoscope

We're all familiar with Aesop's fable of the tortoise and the hare, in which a plodding tortoise manages to win a race against a speedier competitor, as a result of its slow and steady persistence. This story is usually rolled out as a morality lesson about the importance of tenacity: Stick to your guns, we're told, and you can win out over those who charge out of the starting gate full of passion and speed but lack staying power.

For astrologers, though, this tale could just as well serve to illustrate an important facet of the planet Saturn – namely, its "late bloomer" quality. We tend to think of planetary principles in terms of static meanings, but it's good to remember that they also manifest through a complex set of developmental dynamics over time.

That's especially true of Saturn, I've come to see. Simply put, whatever it touches in the horoscope tends to reach true potential only after years of struggle and maturation. One way or another, for better or worse, Saturn's full effects unfold very s-l-o-w-l-y. This doesn't mean that Saturn can't lead to remarkable achievements early on, because it sometimes can – like the person with Saturn conjunct Mercury who shows signs of intellectual genius from a young age. But even in these cases, we'll tend to see enormous hard work and effort being applied, or that early brilliance will ripen into something deeper and different as the years progress. Either way, it's an expression of the gradual dynamic characterizing this planet.[1]

I've come to believe that understanding this dynamic is critical toward not only grasping the role of Saturn in the chart, but also unlocking the entire horoscope itself. Why? In a way, it goes back to some of the very things we normally dislike about this planet: hard work, struggle, recurring obstacles, and so forth. By way of contrast, whatever Jupiter touches tends to indicate where things come relatively easily and flow more naturally. Saturn is not like that. Whatever it touches is where you usually have to work hard for whatever you get, and you can face major hurdles just to reach "the finish line." There's a silver lining, though, and it's this: The sheer amount of hard work you apply to that area can bring about a level of mastery you probably wouldn't have gained otherwise – and that, in turn, can affect everything else in your life. No small matter.

In this article, we'll explore how the late-bloomer influence of Saturn can affect the other planets in one's horoscope. As far as aspects are concerned, it goes without saying that the stressful contacts to Saturn (square, opposition, and often the conjunction) are the most challenging of all, yet they also increase the potential for failure or success in those areas. (That's especially true of the conjunction, which seems to bring out both the best and the worst in Saturn at once.) What I'll be laying out here are primarily best-case scenarios, showing what can result if a person learns to channel these energies in the most constructive way possible. Whether someone actually chooses to go that route is difficult to say, since it hinges on many things, but we can do our best as astrologers to encourage that possibility.[2] That said, let us turn our attention now to Saturn's influence on the largest body in our solar system.

Saturn–Sun

I call this connection *the struggle to shine*. The Sun in the horoscope symbolizes our essential identity and the impulse to express that character before the world. When Saturn is closely involved with the Sun, it makes for a more strenuous effort in forging our public or professional identity, or in gaining respect for that creative light. We may feel blocked in that effort, as though we're standing in the shadow of others, whether that be a prominent or powerful parent, more successful peers or co-workers, or even an intimidating boss. For that reason, I've sometimes referred to the Sun/Saturn combo as the "Rodney Dangerfield" aspect, after the late comedian who gained fame for the line "I don't get no respect!"

The silver lining here is that that sense of frustration compels us to work that much harder to "prove" ourselves and step out from behind those long shadows toward greater respect. Remember, there's almost always a strong element of "compensation" involved with Saturn: Whatever it touches can be where we feel somehow inadequate or even inferior, and we are prompted to struggle even harder to make up for it.

It's like the old Avis car rental commercial from years back, when the company was trying to compete with Hertz: "We try harder!" Finally, after much constructive effort, individuals with this aspect finally step out from those shadows and into the spotlight, to be honored for who they really are.

A classic example of this dynamic is Beatle George Harrison, who had the Sun and Saturn squaring one another. He often hinted at the frustrations of being in the shadow of both John and Paul, but he eventually achieved acclaim not only for songs like "Something" (called by Frank Sinatra one of the greatest songs ever written), but also for solo albums like *All Things Must Pass*. In a fitting synchronistic touch, the name of his own record label was Dark Horse!

A similar example can be seen in Rolling Stone guitarist Keith Richards, who was born with an opposition between Saturn and the Sun, and who worked for decades in the shadow of his extraverted bandmate, Mick Jagger (a Leo). In recent years, though, Richards has gained increasing attention for his work, not only as a solo artist but through the success of his autobiography, *A Life*.

Other famous individuals with Sun–Saturn connections: Salvador Dalí, Jeff Bridges, and David Carradine (square); Sting and Guru Maharaj-Ji (conjunction); Steven Spielberg (sesquiquadrate).

Saturn–Moon

This one can be called *the struggle to relate*. Whereas the Sun is more professional and public in its expression, the Moon is more private and personal in tone, manifesting largely through emotional connections with friends, family, or partners. When the Moon comes into close contact with Saturn, the result can be serious inhibitions or blockages in forging emotional bonds, as well as in receiving nurturance from others. This is arguably the most difficult of all Saturn combinations, yet even here there is much room for improvement. For example, the sheer pain of dealing with this energy early on sometimes causes the person to eventually work through those emotional blocks using therapeutic methods or spiritual work of some kind, or through channeling those energies into some symbolically meaningful avenue. Consider my female client who suffered terribly as a result of being adopted into an unloving family, but she later vowed to make up for it by showering her own children and grandchildren with affection, working hard to become (in her words) a "model parent." The pain she experienced as a child made her more aware of the pain in others, which she sought to heal – a good example of the more positive side of compensation.

Sometimes food can be the pivotal symbol reflecting the energies of the Moon. One client spoke about being homeless and near starvation at times during his childhood, which compelled him as an adult to enroll in cooking classes at a culinary school. He eventually became a master chef in a major restaurant, where he now donates a certain amount of leftover food to down-and-out people at a homeless shelter. He has Saturn opposing his Moon.

I've noticed that a surprising number of my creatively gifted clients also have a marked Saturn–Moon connection in their horoscope. I suspect some of that may be due to the insecurity this pattern brings, which causes them to seek out public approval in later years. Perhaps they felt starved for attention early on, and now they're going to try to get "fed" by the world in other ways.

Another possibility is that the Saturn–Moon energy has the effect of drawing these individuals inward in ways that prove useful for their creative work or reflection. And over the long run, the sheer frustrations brought on by this pattern early in life can become so pent-up that these people really have to find an outlet of some sort later on, simply to keep a grip on their sanity. As one musician who has this aspect said to me, during his childhood he felt as though his emotions were completely bottled up, but when he writes or performs music nowadays, it's like a cork is being taken out of the bottle and its contents being released into the open air.

Others who have Saturn–Moon connections: Bob Dylan (conjunction); Jack Nicholson and the Dalai Lama XIV (opposition).

Saturn–Mercury

This one might be called *the struggle to communicate*. I know of no better story to illustrate this combination than the life of legendary Greek orator Demosthenes. According to Plutarch, Demosthenes experienced great difficulty speaking publicly while young, because of both a speech impediment and breathing difficulties, which caused him to talk in staggered, clipped sentences. But in classic late-bloomer style, he tackled this problem by working on his diction and projection, using such unorthodox means as speaking with stones in his mouth and shouting into the surf. The end result was that he became what some regarded as history's greatest orator. One doesn't get much more Saturn–Mercury than that!

The "sleeping prophet" Edgar Cayce had Saturn and Mercury conjunct when he was born, and his talents as a medium and metaphysical teacher unfolded relatively late in life. Individuals with this planetary combination frequently have the potential to become profound thinkers, with an ability to reflect deeply on life's big questions. Yet, strangely, even with the so-called harmonious aspects, these people often suffer from a deep sense of inferiority about their communication skills or even their intelligence. Because of their slow and deliberate way of pondering problems, perhaps, they can mistake their own slowness for stupidity – and occasionally, others do, too. Albert Einstein also had Mercury conjunct Saturn and was thought to be mentally slow as a child. We all know how that one turned out.

As a way to compensate for that sense of inadequacy, these individuals can work hard to "bootstrap" their way up into intellectual respectability, often through self-education and extensive reading. Abraham Lincoln had Saturn square his Mercury and rode this energy all the way from a log cabin in Kentucky to the presidency of the United States, studying books every step of the way. Such people also have an uncanny ability to distill into a few words ideas that others take entire volumes to lay out – Lincoln's Gettysburg Address is a beautiful example of that (while Einstein is remembered most famously for even less than that – a simple equation, $E=Mc^2$!).

Others with Saturn–Mercury aspects: Isaac Newton (square), Marlon Brando (opposition); Tina Fey (conjunction), Grandma Moses and the writer David Foster Wallace (conjunction).

Saturn–Venus

I call this one *the struggle to love*. Saturn–Venus connections are notorious for creating roadblocks in someone's romantic life, and though that's often true, this combination can also lead to lasting partnerships, while also conferring a much deeper understanding of love than most will ever know. By analogy, who has a greater appreciation of water – the person swimming in the sea off Fiji, or the person crawling through the desert sands toward an oasis? When Saturn–Venus people finally do discover love, they taste it with a richness that can be truly profound.

I sometimes call this pairing the "ugly duckling" aspect, because of how it affects a person's experience of their own beauty over time. Venus has much to do with personal charm: How refined and ingratiating are you when dealing with others? How alluring do you appear to the world? The answers to these questions hinge to a great degree on the condition of your Venus. When Saturn is involved with Venus, it can therefore make people with this pairing feel gawky or insecure about their attractiveness early on, even to the point of feeling ugly or coarse (especially in the case of the hard aspects). Though they sometimes present an aloof front to the world, inwardly they may be feeling like an outcast, someone who has been "left out."

But as these individuals mature and learn to break out from their shell, they become far more comfortable in their own skin, and others start seeing them differently, too. Think here of Eliza Doolittle in *My Fair Lady* and the work that went into making her a "proper" lady. Or consider the real-life case of Princess Diana, who had a trine between these planets and ripened from a skinny, shy girl into a symbol of glamour in her final years. (Having a late-bloomer chart doesn't necessarily guarantee longevity, by the way! It's always proportional to the life you do live, whether that be to age 9 or 90.)

When it comes to money, the late-bloomer side of Saturn–Venus can manifest as the "rags to riches" syndrome, where a person goes from relative scarcity to considerable affluence later in life. Look at some of the economic heavy-hitters with a strong pairing of Saturn and Venus: Bill Gates (conjunction), Jeff Bezos of Amazon.com (conjunction), and Oprah Winfrey (square), to name just three. When a square or opposition is involved, it can lead to major ups and downs in someone's financial fortunes, of course, but it doesn't necessarily deny the fortune itself.

Venus also plays a part in creativity, so when paired with Saturn this sometimes makes for a slow-unfolding dynamic in someone's artistic development. Famed architect Frank Lloyd Wright had a tight opposition between Saturn and Venus, and in addition to his notoriously checkered love life, by many accounts he experienced the most fruitful phase of his career between the ages of 70 and 90.

Other individuals with Saturn–Venus connections: Michelangelo and Joni Mitchell (square); Georgia O'Keefe (sextile), Lord Byron, Auguste Rodin, and John F. Kennedy, Jr. (all with the conjunction).

Saturn–Mars

Simply put, this is *the struggle for courage*. Some of us remember the ads from our childhood comic books about the 97-pound weakling who gets sand kicked in his face by the bully at the beach, but goes on to become a body-building marvel who can stand up to anybody. That's not a bad depiction of the Saturn–Mars dynamic. As a result of feeling insecure about their assertiveness or physical strength, these individuals often wind up working that much harder to develop their muscles, figuratively or literally, and can become surprisingly powerful in the process.

One of my male clients with a conjunction between these planets was tormented as a child by a neighborhood bully, who constantly called him "wimp." This led him to begin an intensive regimen of martial arts training, and he eventually earned a black belt in karate. A similar dynamic is portrayed in the film *Rocky*, where Sylvester Stallone's character manages, through sheer grit and determination, to climb his way from underdog status up through the prizefighting ranks toward respect and prestige. Bruce Lee, who was born with an opposition between Mars and Saturn, worked his way back from a crippling injury to become arguably the most famous martial artist of the 20th century.

Another real-life example of this pattern is writer Ernest Hemingway, who had Saturn square Mars. As a child, he was surrounded primarily by women, and his mother even sometimes dressed him up in frilly girl's clothing. One doesn't have to be a world-class psychologist to realize there may have been compensation behind Ernest's macho posturing as an adult, including his well-known penchant for boxing and big-game hunting. Yet, for all of that, those who knew him well attested that he was a genuinely courageous figure who showed no fear in the face of danger (an attitude that may have stemmed partly from an out-of-body experience he had on the battlefield during World War I). Rightly or wrongly, for many of his generation, Hemingway became a living symbol of courage and virility – quite a contrast to the girlish "mama's boy" this sensitive Cancer seemed just as likely to become early on.

Others with Saturn–Mars connections: Charles Atlas (conjunction), Ted Turner (opposition); Michelangelo, Jack LaLanne and John Dillinger (trine).

Saturn–Jupiter

We can label this one *the struggle for meaning*. Here, the slow-developing dynamic of Saturn tends to express itself in spiritual or ideological ways. Consider the example of my friend who was raised in an ultra-religious environment, which had the unintended result of causing her to disavow religion entirely and become a "borderline atheist" in her 20s. But like a prodigal child returning to the fold, she slowly rediscovered religion and eventually became an ordained pastor herself. When friends from her 20s meet her now, she says, they can't believe she's the same person they knew back in the old days. It's worth mentioning that some believe that both Buddha and Jesus had this conjunction in their horoscopes; if so, that would fit this dynamic well, since both broke free from their received religions in order to form their own spiritual traditions.

In a more general way, Jupiter governs one's opinions and beliefs, as well as the urge to express these to the world. The combination of Jupiter and Saturn is therefore one of the chief indicators of a spiritual teacher or professor. Beatle John Lennon had the conjunction between these planets; he not only underwent major shifts in his attitude toward religion (think back to his falling out with the Maharishi, for one), but also wound up experiencing enormous backlash for his public comments on religion. When he said in 1965 that the Beatles are "more popular than Jesus," it led to protests around the world from religious followers and leaders, who misinterpreted the comment completely. In some ways, Lennon is now remembered almost as much for his political and spiritual views as for his musical output.

Individuals born with this combination can be forced at times to take a stand regarding their ideological principles, in ways that might entail sacrifice or setbacks. Yet, ultimately, such challenges often have the effect of strengthening their moral resolve, or can even lead to greater things later on. Early in his career, African-American actor Sidney Poitier (with the square) was offered an acting role that he felt was demeaning to blacks, so he refused it – despite the fact that he and his wife desperately needed money. But as difficult as this choice was, he knew it was the right thing to do and later described it as a turning point in his moral growth, while also pointing out how it paved the way to better acting roles.

Jupiter also governs institutions of higher learning. One client of mine with Saturn–Jupiter square described being sidetracked from obtaining a degree during her college years, then eventually going back to school in her early sixties to finally obtain that much-sought diploma. As is often the case, the Saturn influence didn't so much deny a dream as delay it – and in her case, that delay gave a deeper appreciation for the real meaning of education and knowledge than most younger students probably ever experience.

A variation on this theme is visible in the life of psychedelic guru Timothy Leary, born with a conjunction between Saturn and Jupiter. Fired from a teaching position at Harvard, he eventually wound up spreading his ideas to a far larger audience than the school ever provided – this (ironically) included going on lecture tours to college campuses across the country. The dicey chemistry between Saturn and Jupiter can also be seen in Leary's lifelong battles with the law and judges, which culminated in various arrests and his serving time in prison.

Others with Saturn–Jupiter combinations: Sigmund Freud (square), Sting (opposition); Krishnamurti and scientist John Lilly (trine); Galileo and Bob Dylan (conjunction).

Saturn–Uranus

This pairing might be called *the struggle for personal freedom*. Uranus governs one's sense of individuality, so when Saturn couples with this planet, there can be a battle between conformity and rebelliousness, between the urge to fit in and the urge to be free. These people can experience repeated problems trying to forge their own idiosyncratic path, in the effort to "do their own thing."

Yet, over time, those same developmental tensions can spur them to develop an even stronger sense of who they are, and such individuals may even become a force for change in the arts, science, or politics.

There's an important lesson here about the value of Saturn, in terms of how the roadblocks it creates force us to become stronger or at least clarify our perspective. And without those restrictive structures to butt up against, we wouldn't develop nearly as clear a sense of our own values or boundaries in that area. As they say, the ringed planet is a hard taskmaster sometimes, but it's a great teacher.

Rock-and-roller Sting has a square between these planets, with Uranus being the focal point of a t-square. In his memoir, *Broken Music*, he describes the frustrations of working in a regimented classroom job teaching at a girl's school, but then throwing caution to the wind by relocating with his family and joining the rock band The Police. But even that began to feel restrictive for him, prompting him to again break free and chart his own course as a solo act. It's been a path of increasing individualism and personal freedom, and it probably wouldn't have happened if Saturn hadn't provided the limitations that prompted Sting to crystallize his personalized vision.

Bob Dylan was born with a conjunction between Saturn and Uranus. Early in his career, he ignited controversy in the musical world by breaking loose from the folk community so he could head off into more personal directions, climaxing in a literally electrified performance at the Newport Folk Festival in 1965. In a still broader way, though, his entire life has been a struggle with the whole issue of freedom, since finding his own personal space in the midst of massive public scrutiny has taken on growing importance. With his natal Moon sandwiched between Uranus and Saturn (a planetary trifecta that can make relationships especially challenging), it's easy to imagine the frustrations he's experienced dealing with the pressures of countless people wanting a piece of his time.

Both Dylan's and Sting's careers illustrate another way the Saturn–Uranus combination can manifest over time – namely, the struggle to reconcile old and new. One may feel torn between the limitations of tradition and innovation and can even teeter-totter at times between these extremes. Yet, sometimes that late-bloomer dynamic can result in an effort to synthesize these opposing forces into an original fusion, reflecting the influences of both old and new simultaneously. In Dylan's case, he didn't abandon traditional musical forms so much as incorporate them into his newer experiments. Likewise, though Sting has worked largely within the rock-and-roll genre, he's managed to introduce progressive and jazz influences into his music along the way, while occasionally dabbling in more traditional musical forms as well, as with his 2009 album, *Songs from the Labyrinth* and his 2014 Broadway musical *The Last Ship*.

Others with Saturn–Uranus aspects: Karl Marx and Dan Rather (square), Elvis Presley (sextile), Barbara Streisand (conjunction).

Saturn–Neptune

This combination might be described as *the struggle to transcend*. Sometimes referred to as symbolizing "the mystic urge," Neptune fuels the desire to escape the shackles of ordinary life in order to pursue loftier ideals or experience more ethereal feelings. The coupling of Saturn with Neptune can therefore bring about disappointments or disillusions as one grows older and discovers that certain closely held dreams and desires are actually illusions – or simply unobtainable.

Yet, that same suffering and disillusionment can bring about a profound sensitizing of the soul, which can then be channeled through creative, spiritual, or social avenues. Consider the case of Swedish director Ingmar Bergman, born with Neptune widely conjunct Saturn; he took the innate pain and heaviness of this aspect and funneled it into brilliant films about life's weightier matters, such as *The Seventh Seal* and *Scenes from a Marriage*. In a way that's similar to Saturn–Moon combinations, the innate pain of hard Neptune–Saturn aspects may further serve to fuel creative activities because of the need to find constructive outlets for bottled-up emotions.

The career of another filmmaker, Kathryn Bigelow, illustrates how this planetary combination can sometimes produce a slow ripening of aesthetic impulses, not unlike Saturn–Venus. A member of the early 1950s generation that had Neptune and Saturn conjunct in their charts, she reached her greatest success at the ripe young age of 58, when she became the first female ever to win an Oscar for Best Director at the 2010 Academy Awards – she's a cinematic late-bloomer, you could say. Saturn rules discipline, so when it is linked with Neptune, there can be extraordinary discipline directed toward other Neptunian arts, too. Fred Astaire had a tight opposition between Saturn and Neptune, and the long years of hard work he devoted to mastering his footwork (Neptune) led to extraordinary success as one of the premier dancers in the world.

For the more sociopolitical side of Saturn–Neptune, we can always look to the case of Abraham Lincoln. Born with a conjunction of these planets, it's clear from his biographies that he experienced considerable suffering early in life, due to assorted professional failures as well as serious relationship issues and bouts of depression. Yet, that same suffering probably fueled the spiritual side of his personality along with the political decisions he'd eventually make. His attitude toward slavery changed considerably over the years, shifting from being ambivalent about it to advocating emancipation. It's not hard to imagine that his growing sympathies on this issue stemmed at least in part from the suffering he himself experienced throughout life.

Neptune also rules drugs, so it's interesting to see how the late-bloomer dynamic of Saturn–Neptune sometimes manifests with clients in terms of their relationship with drugs or alcohol. At least two of my clients with tight Saturn–Neptune aspects went from being heavy drug users in their younger years to becoming drug counselors, and both are now clean and sober.

Others with Saturn–Neptune connections: Cecil B. DeMille (conjunction); J. S. Bach, Mozart, and Václav Havel (all with the opposition).

Saturn–Pluto

One might well call this aspect *the struggle to overcome*. Pluto is similar to Mars – both are concerned with sexuality, raw power, and matters of control – but with a subtle difference: Pluto's power is more covert and subterranean in expression, so whereas Mars might be likened to a stick of dynamite, Pluto is more like a coiled-up serpent. That compressed quality gives Pluto even more power than Mars – for either good or ill.

Add Saturn to that mix, and it's like clamping down on that Plutonian serpent, tightening that already compressed energy – making the potentials for constructive or destructive manifestations that much stronger. For these individuals, the presence of Pluto–Saturn in their lives can often feel as though they're being forced to contend with titanic challenges. But with that struggle can emerge a degree of willpower that seems almost superhuman at times. These people can move mountains, if they put their mind to it.

Consider the example of Arnold Schwarzenegger, who was born with a conjunction between Saturn and Pluto. It's well known that

Schwarzenegger faced obstacles in his youth that would have stymied most mere mortals, including an impossibly long and guttural name, a thick accent, freakishly angular features, and questionable acting skills, at best. Yet, he prevailed over those challenges to succeed in various careers as a body builder, real estate developer, and box-office megastar – marrying into a prominent family (the Kennedys) and, last but not least, getting elected to a high office in the United States. With each hurdle, his psychological muscles seemed to become stronger and more durable. In fact, there's some affinity here with his signature movie character, *The Terminator*: Both share that indomitable drive so common to Saturn–Pluto that keeps them coming back time and again, no matter what gets thrown at them.

We also see this pattern in Ernest Hemingway's horoscope, as part of a t-square involving the Saturn–Mars aspect mentioned earlier. Hemingway rebounded from various tragedies and brushes with death, and his Nobel Prize–winning novel, *The Old Man and the Sea*, embodied the Saturn–Pluto dynamic to a "T." It tells of an old man matching wits with a powerful creature of the deep, but persevering in the end and finally towing the tattered remains of his prey back to safe harbor. The story has sometimes been compared to *Moby Dick*, by the way, which tells its own tale of someone doing battle against a huge creature – and not too surprisingly, Herman Melville had Saturn and Pluto aligned as well (conjunct).

There's no escaping it: Pluto involves sexuality, too. So, when Saturn joins hands with it, the dynamics of passion become complicated at times, maybe even explosive. Famed lothario Warren Beatty was born with these planets trine, and his first major "breakout" role was in the Elia Kazan classic, *Splendor in the Grass*, playing a sexually repressed young man.[3] Surprisingly, there's some resonance between this screen character and Beatty's own life, since he supposedly remained a virgin until age 20 – then apparently spent the next 30 years making up for lost time. When the power of Pluto is unleashed, it is indeed a force to be reckoned with.

Others with Saturn–Pluto connections: Friedrich Nietzsche, Bruce Lee (square), James Dean (opposition); Walt Whitman, Alan Watts, Orson Welles, Oliver Stone, Jack Lalanne, and David Letterman (all with the conjunction).

Final Remarks

We've seen just a few of the ways Saturn can influence the planets in one's horoscope, although we could also look to the house or sign placements of Saturn, any planets in Capricorn, and the houses Capricorn falls on. In other words, all Saturn-related energies in the horoscope tend to have a late-blooming quality to them, unfolding far more slowly over time.

For example, Saturn in the 7th house may seem to deny marriage or partnership (which is exactly what some of the older astrological texts ominously portend), yet in reality, it more often simply delays it. And in so doing, it sometimes opens the door to a stronger marital bond than if the person had exchanged vows earlier on, like everyone else in their circle. Going back to our earlier example, Warren Beatty was notoriously shy about committing himself in relationship during his early years, but he finally surprised everyone by tying the knot with Annette Bening when he was in his 50s! By all accounts, they've managed to raise a happy family in one of the most divorce-prone areas of the U.S. – Hollywood.

Similarly, Venus in Capricorn, Saturn in Libra, or Capricorn on the 7th house may produce struggles or frustrations with partnerships early on but with the long-range possibility of greater success in forging stable, satisfying relationships – sometimes as a result of having learned the hard way what not to do. In any event, one has to carefully study the aspects involved to truly grasp the likelihood of either success or failure, and to zero in on what challenges the client most needs to work on.

One last thing: I feel that understanding this side of Saturn's influence is important for refining not only how we interpret charts but also how we counsel our clients. Countless times through the years, I've watched as clients became visibly relieved to hear that the struggles they've been dealing might well lessen with time, or lead to successful outcomes. As one young client with both Saturn and Capricorn prominent said to me after our session, "The most valuable thing I got out of this reading today was simply hearing that it's going to get better. I've been thinking that my entire life is going to remain this hard, so just knowing there could be a light at the end of the tunnel makes me feel like a weight has been lifted off my shoulders." That's not an atypical comment by any stretch. We shoulder great responsibility as astrologers in helping clients to reframe the challenges in their lives, in helping them to see those problems in a more positive light. Grasping the late-bloomer dimensions of Saturn, I believe, offers an especially valuable tool toward that end.

Notes

1. With a little help from famed astrologer Alan Leo, British composer Gustav Holst displayed uncanny insight into the archetypal nature of the planets when he composed his popular orchestral suite, *The Planets*. Listen, for instance, to his composition "Saturn: Bringer of Old Age," and you'll hear the slowly unfolding, late-bloomer dynamic in exquisite action: The work begins at a plodding pace, heavy as cement and morose as a funeral, but midway through, it shifts gears and blossoms into a spaciously beautiful cascade of strings – still slow and slightly "heavy" in tone, yet transformed by a sweetness that is almost Venusian. All of Holst's planetary passages are beautifully conceived, but to my mind there are special insights to be gleaned from his take on the ringed planet, which echoes the ancient symbol of the cornucopia – namely, that hidden riches sometimes lie within the brittle, somber shell of Saturn.

2. How can we tell whether or not someone will express the more constructive qualities of a dominant Saturn? That's an immensely complicated question and can hinge on many things. For example, I know two people born around the same time and date, with very similar horoscopes and both with Saturn–Neptune–Venus conjunctions in Libra. The one person has taken that energy and become a successful musician, while the other has sadly drifted into a life of alcoholism and self-pity, largely over failed relationships. What made the difference? The only major distinction I can make out between their horoscopes was that the first person had a more powerful Jupiter (closely trining the Moon), which possibly gave her more positivity and resilience for coping with the difficulties of Saturn. But whether that's the key factor is impossible to say for sure, since some individuals overcome their challenging horoscopes even without the benefit of supportive aspects. In the end, it seems to come down to that mysterious factor called "attitude" – and that may or may not be something ultimately encoded in the chart.

3. Oddly enough, Beatty's second major breakout role in the film industry, as Clyde Barrow in the 1967 film *Bonnie and Clyde*, was again as a

sexually frustrated figure. It's ironic that a sexually notorious figure like Beatty would rise to fame through such libido-challenged roles, but it's reminiscent of that other Saturn–Pluto figure, Ernest Hemingway. He, too, gained fame for being associated with a sexually impotent character: Jake Barnes in Hemingway's first novel, *The Sun Also Rises*.

Reprinted from *The Mountain Astrologer*, October/November 2010.

4

The Seven Most Common Mistakes Made by Astrologers

Anyone who has interpreted horoscopes professionally for any length of time has no doubt experienced their own learning curve as to what is – and isn't – effective when working with clients. As most of us have come to realize, a careless piece of advice or bit of counseling can have long-term effects on the life-direction or emotional well-being of a client, for better or worse.

So what are the most serious mistakes astrologers tend to make with their clients? Having made my fair share of them over the years (while also having the benefit of observing other astrologers at work!), I've put together a short list of what I believe are among the more common problems astrologers should be on guard for. Here they are:

1) *Starting off your consultation with something negative*. This one seems simple, but it's actually a biggie. Years ago one of my first astrology teachers offered me this advice: "Whatever you do, make sure the first thing you say during a reading is positive, especially if it's a first-time client." I asked why. "Because if you start off with a negative comment, that's all they'll probably hear and they'll go away thinking how dire or downbeat your reading was."

This is one mistake I learned about early myself, in fact. The very first astrologer I ever spoke with, when I was just 18, began our discussion with something slightly ominous about my future. Even though they went on to say other, more positive things during the reading, by that point I was so bothered by his opening salvo that it largely eclipsed everything else he said. It wasn't until a full year later that I finally worked up the nerve to seek out a more experienced astrologer for a second opinion; to my relief, they explained how the previous astrologer (a relative beginner) had used the entirely wrong birth year when calculating my horoscope, so was using a mistaken chart! Had I never gone to another astrologer, I would have gone on for years believing what he said about my destiny; but I'm also convinced that had he inserted those critical comments later on in the reading, rather than opening with them, they would have packed far less punch than they did.

2) *Telling people what to do*. On more than one occasion, I've had a client ask me whether they should marry such-and-such a person, or move to another part of the country, or some other life-changing question. But is it really our job to make up our client's minds for them and decide the important actions in their lives? As I'll explain in more detail in chapter 7, that may not be very smart. Spiritually speaking, it not only deprives them of an important element of free choice – remember Star Trek's "Prime Directive" of non-interference? – but it can actually set them off in the wrong direction since we've based our counsel on the context of our own life-perspective, not theirs. Rather, our job as astrologers is to provide as much sound feedback as we can about their choices, but leave the final decision up to them (unless, of course, you're eager to take on that load of extra karma from them following your advice!).

This same advice holds for interpreting birth charts. One of my very first chart sessions was for someone with an extensive background in therapy, and who was psychologically savvy as a result. At one point I began focusing on an especially difficult configuration in his horoscope involving planets in the 10th house. Not being content to simply describe the dynamics of that pattern, I went the extra step of telling them how they need to be "less ambitious" and "career-driven," and learn to focus more on their domestic life – in other words, telling them how they should act.

My client calmly took issue with this, explaining why he disagreed with the "curative" approach to counseling in general. It's one thing to try and shed light on someone's issues, he argued, but quite another to tell them, authoritatively, what they should do, how they should act, how they need to be, and so on. It's easy for many of us in a counseling line of work to fall prey to the "rescue" mindset, of thinking we need to jump in and change the client somehow, or impose our value system onto them. More often than not, such impulses are driven by unconscious needs of our own, relating to unresolved issues we haven't come to terms that we're now trying work out through them, by "proxy." To put it simply, our job is not to change our client, but to help make change possible.

3) *Not being sufficiently informed about why a client came to you in the first place*. During the early years, I sometimes had the experience of finishing up what I thought was a superb, first-class reading – only to dis-

cover towards the very end that I didn't even touch on what they came for. I spent an hour elucidating the marvelous subtleties of their psyche and their karmas, only to discover that what they really wanted to know about was their prospects for finding true love.

So whenever I begin my sessions now I'm careful to ask, "What did you come here for?" Or, "What are you most hoping to learn from this session? Is it about romance? Or career? Or something else altogether?" This doesn't mean you can't discuss anything besides those requested points, of course; after all, there may be a reason they were paired up with you in the first place that's completely separate from their conscious intentions. But from a professional standpoint it's only fitting that you provide them with the service they're paying their hard-earned money for.

4) *Using jargon.* Imagine walking into a someone's office and they start saying, "Well, your zargon is squaring your wiggleshank, and your alpharop is in stressful relation to your kokomo in the seventh-domain. That's important!" No, that's gobbly-gook. But it's exactly how our counseling can sometimes sound to a non-astrologer when we insist on using insider terminology.

I have to confess I'm not a purist on this point since I feel there are times when some terminology is helpful, presuming the client has a basic knowledge of astrology. In those cases, coupling your remarks with a basic reference to the planetary symbols at work can actually fast-track your discussion nicely in some ways, since the person will automatically have a grasp of the archetypal implications involved. But ultimately that's something each astrologer has to decide for themselves, since it hinges on the knowledge and openness of the client. But for the most part, too many beginning astrologers fail to realize when they've crossed that fine line between clarity and obtuseness, when falling back on jargon may actually be an excuse for not fully understanding the meaning of the patterns yourself.

5) *Overly simplistic or judgmental interpretations.* Though I'd like to think most of us have long since moved past the stage of black-or-white renderings that were more common in the old days ("Saturn squaring your Mercury means you will die on the gallows!"), I continue to be surprised

by how even many advanced practitioners continue falling into the trap of simplistic interpretations. It may take subtler forms now, like looking at someone's natal Jupiter/Sun square and simply telling them they have a problem with their ego – and leaving it at that. Or noticing a Saturn/Moon opposition and telling the client they may be depressed or emotionally blocked – while completely overlooking the potentially constructive qualities this pattern can bring about, such as emotional gravitas, or compassion born of early suffering. (It was immensely reassuring for one Buddhist client of mine to learn that the Dalai Lama himself also had this aspect!)

This is what I call the "this-means-that" approach to interpretation, as though a given symbol or configuration means just one thing, and one thing only. You have Jupiter in the 9th? Well, you'll have positive experiences with travel or higher education. Simple, eh? You have a retrograde Venus? Well, you're unlucky in love. Too bad. The fact is, planets and aspects are multivalent symbols with many levels of significance and shades of meaning, and while there may not be time to delve into each one of these fully, there can be an even bigger danger when touching on them too superficially. While you don't want to be too vague, don't hamstring your client with the straightjacket of literal meanings, either!

6) *Not giving the client a sense of hope or any constructive options for dealing with the challenges in their horoscope.* When I was first starting out as an astrologer, I had one client arrive with a particularly challenging horoscope, centering on a t-square between the Moon, Venus and a 5th house Saturn. I spoke to them at length about the subtleties of the configuration, going into brilliant detail about all psychological and practical manifestations of this difficult pattern, and felt quite proud of my diamond-sharp insights. But when I was finished, I couldn't help but notice they looked a little dejected, so I asked if there were any questions or comments about what I'd told them. At which point he asked, almost with a hint of exasperation, "Okay…but what am I supposed to do with all that?"

That was a sobering wake-up call for me, because I realized that I hadn't really been offering my clients enough constructive suggestions about their difficult patterns, which probably left more than a few of them feeling a bit confused, or even hopeless. While we don't want to make up their minds for them, it's important that we offer the client options or practical suggestions about how they can respond to their challenges, whether that take the form of therapy, spiritual practice, or specific actions or rituals that can channel or counteract those difficult energies. It's not good enough to simply tell them how difficult things are; we need to provide them with choices, too.

7) *Overlooking the larger patterns in the chart — a.k.a. "missing the forest for the trees."* A few years ago a client came to me wanting a second opinion about what was happening in her life, after a previous astrologer failed to find anything that explained the enormous difficulties she was experiencing at work, primarily with her boss. It didn't take long before I learned what the problem was, or why the other astrologer had missed what seemed so obvious now: they had based their forecast strictly on a computer-generated "hit-list" of transits showing the day-by-day litany of planetary energies, but which didn't emphasize the larger trends in effect at the time.

Specifically, Saturn had moved into this woman's 10th house one year earlier, and would continue to remain there for at least another year; but the astrologer's hit-list was set up only to show only the dates when planets made aspects, as well as when the slower-moving planets first entered houses. Had that astrologer simply taken a step back to actually look at this woman's birth chart to see where those current transiting planets fell along the wheel, he would have realized the importance of this roughly two-year phase in her life as Saturn traversed the 10th house.

A similar problem often crops up when looking at the transits of the outer bodies to one's natal planets. Because they move so slowly, Neptune, Uranus, Pluto, or Saturn can be ten degrees or even more away from the client's Sun or Moon, say, and yet that client will often feel this transit long before it actually becomes exact. (For example, how many Sun-sign Aries, even late-degree ones, felt a marked shift of energy in their lives the very week – or even day – that Uranus moved into their sign back in 2011?) Yet such trends won't show up on many computerized hit-lists, since they're configured to show only a detailed view of what's happening. Consequently, it can be a good idea to visually study the horoscope to see where those transiting bodies actually are within the horoscope, not only in terms of the houses and angles, but in relation to how they are to the natal planets. We can become so focused on the minutia of transiting and progressed positions that we miss the prover-bial "forest for the trees."

These, then, are a few of the problems that can crop up in our dealings with clients, although there are doubtless many others. The moral of the story? It pays to be careful when offering advice or counsel that can have a serious impact on people's lives!

Reprinted from *The Mountain Astrologer*, April/May 2012.

5

What Goes Around Comes Around: Learning from Past Transits to Better Understand Future Trends

For those of us who engage in predictive astrology of any sort, one of the greatest challenges is determining how an upcoming aspect will manifest. It's easy enough to grasp the broader archetypal contours of Saturn crossing over someone's Moon, say, but what if you wish to know more precisely how that upcoming trend will materialize? And what prescriptive measures should we offer a client if we see a difficult trend coming up and they ask for ways of counterbalancing those energies?

I'd like to look here at a simple technique many of us are probably familiar with already but which we may not always take full advantage of. I'm referring to the practice of looking backwards to see what happened during previous passes of a transit to better understand what might occur during upcoming contacts between those bodies. To illustrate what I mean, let's take a look at a few case histories.

The Teacher

I recently had a woman come to me who was about to experience her fourth Jupiter return at age 48. It was natally positioned in Gemini in her 9th house, so I wasn't too surprised to learn she was a professor at a local college. But what would this upcoming Jupiter conjunction bring for her?

Based on the symbolism of these placements, there were many possibilities, of course – publishing, traveling, teaching, religious studies, and so on. But I wanted to pin it down a more specifically, if at all possible. So I asked her if she remembered what happened twelve years earlier, specifically when Jupiter last came around to that same spot?

Fortunately, she remembered clearly, and said she received an award for her teaching at that time. In addition, she also went on a long-distance trip to Japan as part of a research project. Pressing her a little bit further,

I asked if she could recall what happened during the Jupiter conjunction prior to that one, when she was just 24. That's when she graduated from college, she explained, and when she went on another important long-distance trip, though that time to Europe.

Based on these tidbits of information, I could safely suggest this could likewise be an important (and positive) period in her teaching career, but also a time when long-distance travels would be likely, not to mention beneficial. As it turned out, she already had a trip booked to South America, a continent she'd never traveled to before. She was somewhat nervous about the trip, however, and it was actually a large part of the reason she looked me up, so was naturally relieved to hear what the horoscope suggested about that time-frame.

The Entrepreneur

Saturn cycles are longer-range in duration than Jupiter ones, so for that reason can trigger more profound, long-lasting developments. Case in point: a year ago a businessman in his sixties came to me with Jupiter and Venus conjunct in his horoscope. In a few months transiting Saturn was going to be conjuncting that natal pair, and he knew just enough about astrology to feel nervous about what this might bring.

I took a look back in the ephemeris to see when that particular transit last occurred in his life, and found it was in 1982. I asked, "Did anything important happen for you back in 1982, on either a professional or a personal front?" He thought for a second then said, "Yes – that's exactly when I started up the company I now run. It was a lot of hard work getting the kinks worked out, and there were some delays at the time, but the business has been running successfully now for nearly 30 years."

I pressed further, "Can you think of any parallels between what was happening back then and what's happening in your life now? For example, are you thinking of making any changes in your business, or even starting up some new business, like you did back then?" He said, "Both, actually. I'm downsizing the business I started back in 1982, and I've just decided to start up a new company. I'm opening up a chain of restaurants in the Midwest, and the first one will be opening later this year. This is a major transition period for me."

That was helpful info, and allowed me to say with some assurance that Saturn might not produce a setback or loss in his life (as he feared) so much as crystallize a major financial undertaking, or a shift in his business responsibilities. I suggested that the upcoming Saturn transit would probably bring much the same thing into his life now as it did for him back then. There would probably be a lot of hard work, possibly even delays, but the outcome would likely be positive for him (especially considering his natal Jupiter/Venus conjunction). As of this writing that seems to be exactly what's transpiring for him.

The Free Spirit
Sometimes, the half-cycles and quarter-cycles of planetary transits can be just as important to look at, especially with the outer planets, since they move so slowly that they might not complete a full revolution during a person's lifetime. As one illustration, consider the woman who came to me when transiting Uranus was about to oppose her natal Sun. To me, this obviously suggested that major changes could soon happen for her, either internally or externally, possibly both.

But what form would they take?

Now in her sixties, she could clearly remember when Uranus conjuncted her Sun 42 years earlier – 180 degrees away from the opposition that was now emerging. I strongly sensed there could be some resonance between that period and this one, as Uranus now moved in to oppose that earlier point from her twenties.

When I asked her what happened back then, she explained how it was a time of radical change in her life: she moved away from home and family for the first time, in order to live across the country. Just as importantly, this also was a time when she decided on the career direction she's remained in until the present day – as an editor.

I asked her whether she was contemplating any major changes during the coming year. It turned out that she was considering another cross-country move, this time to the American Northwest. But she was also considering taking the literary skills she'd been accumulating since the Uranus/Sun conjunction four decades earlier, and using them to finally become a creative writer herself. So rather than just assist others with their creative work, this was a time she could finally break out and give expression to her own literary voice.

Putting all this info together, I suggested that the current Uranus opposition was in some way a culmination of that earlier time in her life, and involved not just a desire for more independence and change but was also motivating her to explore her own creative potentials as a writer. Based on all she related to me, I could safely encourage her to pursue those creative dreams further. Those opposing points in the Uranian cycle over four decades of time seemed almost like successive acts in a life-long stage play, and explaining it to her in this way seemed to help give her perspective on the course her life was taking.

A Lesson in Anger Management

Finally, an example from my own life. Not long ago I was facing a transiting conjunction of Saturn over my natal Mars. What would this bring? Would it manifest as exhaustion, or as a frustration of my desires? Might I even hit my head if I wasn't careful (something that's happened to me far too often, unfortunately)? How might I best prepare for this energy?

I couldn't clearly remember what happened 30 years earlier when this conjunction last fired, but since I kept a scrupulous daily diary back then, I could go back and read what happened for me during that period in considerable detail.

There were a number of things which happened then, but perhaps the most dramatic was an upsetting confrontation with a truck driver while I was driving in my local neighborhood. I was on my way to attend a class when a large truck directly in front of me decided to make a wide turn to enter a corporate driveway. It abruptly came to a stop, blocking all lanes of traffic in the process. Because I was already late for my class, after waiting 20 or 30 seconds I impatiently decided to honk my horn, which in turn prompted the driver behind me to honk his horn as well.

Upon hearing this, the truck driver proceeded to climb down out of his cab, walk up to my car window, and grab me by the shirt lapel while letting loose with a string of obscenities. He was angry, to put it mildly, and seemed about to punch me in the face. This wasn't going well. Fortunately, I managed to calm him down with a forced smile and some friendly words, at which point he relaxed a bit and let go of my shirt. Through clenched jaw, he muttered how there was another vehicle blocking the driveway he was trying to enter, which I couldn't see from where I was, so he was stuck, too. He seemed just as frustrated by the delay as I was, and was understandably upset at the drivers behind him honking their horns.

The experience shook me up, since it could have easily turned violent, but what I took away from it was the importance of not reacting impulsively, and the need to be more aware of my own impatience in situations. Nothing wrong with honking one's horn, to be sure – I've seen them save lives on occasion – but thinking back on that occasion, I know I wasn't being as careful as I could have been, and could have waited a bit longer to see what was going on before relying on the car horn.

So what did this tell me as I watched Saturn coming around to cross over my Mars again? For one, I knew this could be a time when I needed to watch my emotions and anger more closely, and not react in a knee-jerk way to annoying situations. When the time finally came, I was definitely on my guard – especially while driving! (Understand, during a pleasant Jupiter aspect one can practically get away with almost anything, but under a stressful Saturn the smallest misstep can sometimes lead to disaster. The lessons the ringed planet imparts are meant to stick!)

As things played out this time around, nothing happened on the streets or highways, but what did happen was similar in symbolic ways. On a few occasions during this period I was around people who made emotionally-charged comments about politics and religion that pushed my buttons in a surprising way. Normally, these would have drawn me into heated debates, perhaps even arguments, and I could have easily let myself become upset. But since I knew what was unfolding in my chart, and remembered what happened the previous time, I chose to watch my emotions more carefully. I calmed down my breathing, and measured my comments in a way that actually proved far more effective in communicating my views than raising my voice and going on the offensive. I learned an important lesson by studying what Saturn taught me that previous time, and it allowed me to transmute these energies into something more constructive.

These are just a few examples of how this approach can be employed to flesh out your understanding of predictive cycles before they happen. If you've never used this approach yourself, you might begin by looking at your own horoscope and seeing if there are major transits happening in your life anytime soon, and if so, take a few moments to see what happened when they last triggered in your life. You might be surprised by the subtle ways the lessons of that period shed light on the situations you're entering into now. What's the old saying by Santayana – "Those who forget the past are condemned to repeat it"? Astrology teaches us to remember the past to better prepare for the future.

Reprinted from *Dell Horoscope* magazine, January 2014.

6

Astrology and the Chakras:
Toward a Sacred Psychology of the Horoscope

Understand that thou art another world in little, and hast within thee the Sun and the Moon, and also the stars.

Origen (185/86–254/55 C.E.)

In this article I would like to explore the exciting possibility of bridging two of history's greatest psychological systems, astrology and the chakras. Conventionally, these two systems have been seen as having little or nothing to do with each other, the former primarily concerning the outer world, or macrocosm, and the latter involving the inner world, or microcosm. In fact, as we shall see, these two systems are really two sides of the same coin, each one complementing the other and thus enhancing our understanding of both.

The basic system of correspondences I will be using here is drawn from teachers I have studied with in the Kriya Yoga lineage.[1] The general system of "chakric horoscopes" and their guidelines for interpretation are my own, developed over more than a decade of working with these basic correspondences. With that said, let us begin by exploring some of the core ideas of chakric philosophy.

What Are the Chakras?
In Sanskrit, the word *chakra* (sometimes spelled "cakra") literally means "wheel." In yogic philosophy, this term refers to the psycho-spiritual centers located along the length of the spine, each of which is associated with a different archetypal principle of consciousness. Although there are literally thousands of chakras situated throughout the subtle body, yogic philosophy normally stresses only seven or eight of these. Let us briefly review these primary points and their planetary associations.

Chakras	Planet	Keywords
(8) Sahasrara	-	The Transcendent, Inspiration
(7) Ajna	Sun	Active Awareness, Higher Will
(6) Chandra	Moon	Reflective Awareness, Memory
(5) Vishudda	Mercury	Thinking, Communication
(4) Anahata	Venus	Harmony, Love
(3) Manipura	Mars	Force, Strength, Control
(2) Svadisthana	Jupiter	Inspiration, Morality
(1) Muladhara	Saturn	Structure, Limitation

Illustration 1

Chakra 1, at the base of the spine, is called *Muladhara*. Its element is earth, and it is governed by the planet Saturn. Psychologically, it concerns one's relationship with the material plane, and the principle of limitation in both its constructive and destructive aspects. In its more unbalanced expression, it governs the drive for survival, as well as such states as greed and fear, while its more balanced expression points to such qualities as practicality and worldly skillfulness (business, science, etc.).

Chakra 2 is called *Svadisthana*. Its element is water, and it is ruled by the planet Jupiter. Psychologically, it is one of the centers concerned with emotions, but also relating to morality and values. At its grosser levels of expression, this center governs escapism and dogmatism, while its more constructive expressions include enthusiasm and religious devotion.

Chakra 3 is called *Manipura*. Its element is fire, and Mars is its governing planet. This chakra rules over emotions in their more dynamic and energetic forms. Thus in its less refined state, it relates to anger and combativeness, and is more positively expressed as strength and assertiveness.

Chakra 4 is called *Anahata*. Its element is air, and its corresponding planet is Venus. The psychological focus is on love, beauty, and allurement, and it governs the capacity for harmony in all romantic and social interactions. In its unbalanced form, it produces a tendency toward hedonism, pleasure-seeking, and excessive "sweetness" of temperament, but when in balance, it can give rise to an exceptional sense of aesthetics and even unselfish love.

Chakra 5 is called *Vishuddha*. Its element is ether, and it is governed by the planet Mercury. This chakra's psychological focus is upon mental self-expression and one's ability to formulate or verbalize thoughts. When unbalanced, it produces chaotic thoughts and/or communications, while its constructive expression tends toward creativity, spiritual thinking and refined communication skills.

Chakra 6 is called *Chandra*, and is ruled by the Moon. Though over-looked in most published discussions of the chakras, Paramahansa Yogananda described this as the feminine polarity of the Ajna chakra, or "third eye" (to be considered next). Its emphasis is upon awareness in its most reflective or introspective mode, and it governs such qualities as nurturing compassion and psychic sensitivity. Its more destructive expressions include the experience of fearfulness, emotional dependency, and a preoccupation with the past.

Chakra 7 is called *Ajna* and is located in the center of the forehead, also known as the "third eye." Its corresponding planet is the Sun, and it governs the principle of pure consciousness in its most active, visionary, and expressive form, as well as the higher will. In its balanced state, it rules creativity, spiritual energy, and self-expression, while in unbalanced form it can manifest as egoism, willfulness, "dry" awareness without compassion, and the drive for attention.

Chakra 8 is called *Sahasrara*, the "crown chakra" or "thousand-petaled lotus," and exists at the top of the head above the other chakras. Whereas the previous Ajna chakra represents the supreme realization of personal divinity (perceived in meditation as a five-pointed star), the Sahasrara rules our point of contact with the transpersonal divine, the level of "God-consciousness." However, because this chakra represents a transcendental point beyond the more personal chakras (and, by inference, their astrological correlates), it is largely dormant for most individuals, and can, for purposes of clarity, be left out of our subsequent discussion.

The Twelve Secondary Chakric States

Thus far we have been looking at the chakras only in their simplest possible description. In fact, most of the chakras possess at least three different aspects, or "faces": feminine (introverted), masculine (extroverted), and spiritual (balanced). In other words, each chakra can be diverted over to either its right side or its left side, or it can be experienced in a perfectly balanced fashion in the very center of the spine. In their right- and left-hand aspects, the chakras are associated with the twelve signs of the zodiac.

In each of these three aspects, the psychological energy of any given chakra will manifest in uniquely different ways. For example, when experienced in its more masculine mode (Gemini), the fifth, or Mercury, chakra will generally manifest as interpersonal communications in the waking world, while its more feminine side (Virgo) will tend toward more internalized thought processes, or perhaps even appear within the dream state. In its balanced state within the central channel, however, Mercury rules the mystical mind, that aspect of mentality which truly communes with spirit.

Some traditional esoteric sources, such as Cornelius Agrippa, expressed much the same idea in the following way: Saturn rules Aquarius by day and Capricorn by night; Jupiter rules Sagittarius by day and Pisces by night; Mars rules Aries by day and Scorpio by night; Venus rules Libra by day and Taurus by night; Mercury rules Gemini by day and Virgo by night; while the Sun and Moon hold rulership over one sign each, Leo and Cancer. Yet it is only in the very center of each chakric level that the energy of that chakra truly manifests in a spiritually-balanced fashion, beyond the dualistic qualities of the zodiacal wheel. In its broadest sense, this shows us that the seven classical planets relate to the twelve signs in a startlingly precise way. One simply spins the zodiac around until they fall into line with these chakric placements, as in the following illustration.

What to do with the three outer planets? Note how they fall into line with the first three chakras, in accordance with the zodiacal signs they are commonly associated with by rulership (see illustration 1). Hence, Pluto equates to the feminine side of the Mars chakra (Scorpio), Neptune to the feminine side of the Jupiter chakra (Pisces), and Uranus to the masculine side of the Saturn chakra (Aquarius). Said another way, they are harmonics of those chakric centers.

48

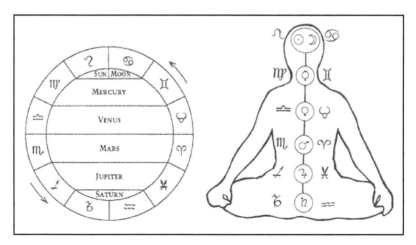

Illustration 2

In yogic philosophy, each of these peripheral chakric compartments represents a sort of memory tract or "storage bin" for karmas and life impressions. Whatever we feel, think, and experience is logged onto the energy fields of the spinal column, both right and left. In this way, habit patterns (or *samskaras*, in yogic terminology) are built up over time, and etched into the subconscious psyche where they continue to compel us toward particular behaviors from life to life. [2]

The Chakric Science of Personality

Every personality is comprised of these basic archetypal elements, although in widely varying combinations. Depending on an individual's karmic patterns, subtle energies concentrate themselves in different areas of the chakric system where they are employed toward either constructive or destructive ends. In this manner, complex patterns are constellated throughout an individual's chakric centers. Although every person experiences all of these centers to one degree or another, certain chakras will be more dominant for some than for others. Hence, an artistic person may have the fourth chakra emphasized, while an intellectual type may have the fifth chakra emphasized, and so forth.

A useful way to illustrate this point is through the notion of *sub-personalities*, since each chakra has its own unique traits or "personifications." Utilizing this system of correspondences, we might describe the different chakras in the following way: the first, or Saturn, chakra can be metaphorically described as the *Inner Politician* or the *Inner Architect*; the second, or Jupiter, chakra is the *Inner Optimist* or the *Inner Preacher*; the third chakra is, plain and simple, the *Inner Warrior*; the fourth, Venus, chakra is the *Inner Lover* or *Inner Artist*; the fifth, or Mercury, chakra is the *Inner Communicator* or *Inner Thinker*; the sixth, or lunar, chakra is the *Inner Mother* or the *Inner Queen*; the seventh, or solar, chakra is the *Inner Father* or the *Inner King*. Certain chakric levels will be emphasized in any given horoscope, and this will determine an individual's dominant sub-personalities.

With this as a foundation, we can begin to explore some of the specific ways a horoscope can reveal a person's chakric energies. Based on my own experience with this system through the years, I believe there are at least three primary levels on which this can be approached, all of which have to be considered in any study of the chakric horoscope. The first of these involves looking at the planets in one's chart and their condition (by aspect or angular strength); the second involves examining the signs and their relative emphases according to planetary placement; the third concerns the houses and their planetary emphasis. Due to space limitations, I will focus here only on the second of these – chakric interpretation using the signs.

We have seen how the twelve signs closely correspond to the different chakras by spinning the zodiac around until Cancer and Leo are positioned at the top of the wheel. The placement of a person's planets within the various signs can provide important clues as to which chakric levels are emphasized. For example, any large constellation of planets in Libra or Taurus would indicate a heavy focus of attention on lessons of the heart, or fourth, chakra, while planets in Scorpio or Aries would indicate a focus of energies on the naval, or third, chakra, and so forth. In theory, these chakric emphases would manifest as energy patterns in those corresponding areas of the person's aura, in turn perceptible to sufficiently clairvoyant individuals.

This kind of interpretation can be refined considerably since each planet is subtly different in how it amplifies a given chakric level. For example, Saturn in one chakra will have a dramatically different effect than if Jupiter is found in that same chakric center. Specifically, where Saturn is placed shows where that person may feel especially challenged to grow, or, in its more frustrating form, where they may feel denied in some way. In a subtler sense, of course, the placement of Saturn indicates the chakric level at which one may also find the greatest depth of wisdom carried over from past lives. In any event, one would probably have to work very hard for desired results in the chakric level inhabited by Saturn, although for that very reason one might also have a much greater appreciation for the rewards of that chakra. By contrast, in whatever chakra Jupiter is placed indicates where one experiences more obvious blessings and good fortune, where there is a more fluid opening and expression of life energies – possibly to excess.

Arguably, the most important significators to look for, chakrically, are the Sun, Moon, and Ascendant. Simply by studying these basic points, one can, I believe, learn a great deal about an individual's chakric focus in this life. For instance, Sun in Gemini would strongly suggest a heightened focus upon the throat chakra of mentality and communication, whereas Sun in Capricorn would point to an intense direction of energies toward the earth plane and the establishment of success, recognition, or simply balance on this level. As most astrologers know, these primary indicators (Sun, Moon, and Ascendant) have their own unique and subtly different shades of meaning – a source of lively debate among astrologers over the years. My own feeling on this matter is that the Moon indicates the chakric level one is *coming from* both emotionally and karmically; the Ascendant shows where the everyday personality in this life is *presently at*, in terms of visible, habitual ways of thinking and relating; and the Sun indicates the chakric direction one is *aspiring toward* in this life, and which one is attempting to bring into creative manifestation.

Five Case Studies

Let's look at a few examples and explore some possible ways this system can be used to understand a person's chakras. All of these horoscopes have been chosen on the basis of unusually dramatic planetary emphases and characteristics, from which the reader may then extrapolate subtler patterns of meaning and methods of interpretation. (Note: Strictly for simplicity's sake, I have not included secondary factors like the nodes, asteroids, or Arabic parts. In all of these chakric horoscopes, where the zodiacal location of the Ascendant is known with any degree of certainty, I have indicated it using the letters "AS.")

In all case studies, the conventional Western horoscope – tropical zodiac/Placidus house cusps – appears above the chakric horoscope.

Case Study #1

Illustration 3 follows on the next page. This is the chakric profile of a writer who specializes in works of a spiritual nature. He is highly prolific, hard-working, and writes in an austere, deeply insightful style. Most notable here is the group of planets located in the Virgo half of the throat (Mercury) chakra. This stellium is in a mercurial sign, and includes the planet Mercury as well, which strongly underscores the importance of this particular chakra in the horoscope. The added fact that his conventional chart shows these planets positioned in the angular 10th house emphasizes this chakra in an even more dramatic way.

What this tells us from a chakric standpoint is that this person possesses an extremely fertile and disciplined mind, suggesting a life directed toward both knowledge and communication. Importantly, Saturn is in orb of a conjunction with Mercury, once again emphasizing the throat chakra. As already noted, there are often struggles and early frustrations in any area touched by Saturn, although this connection usually indicates a considerable depth of knowledge and discipline in those same areas. As might be expected with Saturn conjunct Mercury in Virgo, his overall approach is comparatively traditional in nature, concerned with championing the importance and value of time-proven ideas and techniques.

Frequently I have found that any major accenting of the throat chakra can indicate an involvement with healing or the health profession. Recall how the symbol of the winged caduceus, now commonly associated with the health profession, is traditionally depicted as held by Hermes (or Mercury), perhaps symbolizing the importance of the mind in healing and the maintenance of chakric equilibrium. Appropriately, this individual is highly knowledgeable regarding Eastern forms of healing and has written extensively on this subject.

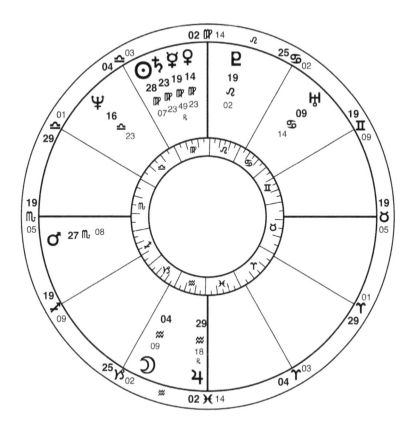

Illustration 3: The Writer. Data withheld.

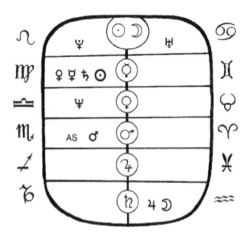

Case Study #2

Illustration 4 follows on the next page. Here we see the chart of an artist. The native is female, and spends the greater part of her time painting, writing, and conducting workshops. Her artwork is spiritual in style and content, with a strong emphasis on color and harmony of line and form. Note the astonishing emphasis on the heart level (fourth chakra): not only is she a Sun in Taurus with Moon in Libra (both Venus-ruled signs), but there are a total of seven planets in Venusian signs. It is hardly surprising that she chooses to express herself through artistic forms. (The reader may notice that she is born in the midst of the Taurus stellium referred to elsewhere in this volume)

It is important when working with this system to avoid assigning labels like "good" or "bad" when evaluating the different chakras. For example, some may be tempted to regard the higher chakras as more intrinsically "spiritual," and the lower chakras as more "negative." In fact, there is no chakra that can't be utilized in either a spiritual or destructive fashion, whether it's positioned high or low on the chakric tree. (Indeed, I find myself agreeing with one colleague who remarked that the longer he is involved with spiritual practice, the more he appreciates the importance of the lower three chakras in maintaining and fueling that practice!) While this woman has obviously used her Venusian energy in a more spiritually-constructive fashion, we might do well to recall, by way of contrast, Adolph Hitler's horoscope, with its strong Taurus Sun and Libra Ascendant, likewise indicating a prominent fourth (Venus) chakra. Hitler nurtured a secret aspiration throughout his life to be an artist, and yet that same energy also produced, in considerably more unbalanced form, a sensibility which valued works of art over human lives, along with a preference for beautifully formed "Aryan" humans. So while it's safe to assume an individual with a prominent heart chakra will be involved with matters of beauty and love, it is quite another matter to determine how they'll choose to express that involvement.

As with conventionally-drawn charts, one of the more telling features of chakric profiles is not simply what they show but what they don't show. Case in point: whenever one finds stelliums or important configurations converging on certain areas, other areas of the horoscope may come up short as a result. Ive often found that one of the challenges for individuals with a prominent Venus chakra, due to their acute sensitivity to harmony and beauty, is learning to deal with the "grosser" energies

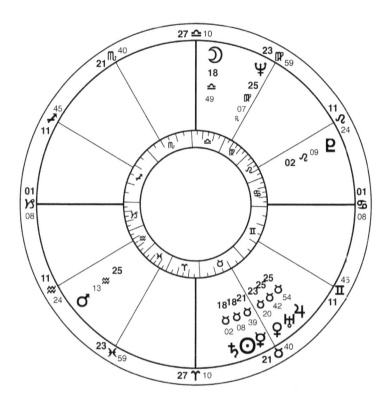

Illustration 4: The Artist. Data withheld.

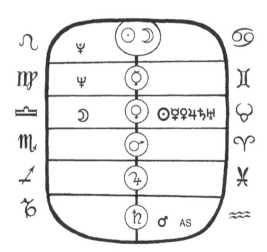

and emotions of the "lower" chakras. This applies to Mars in particular, and its corresponding issues of assertiveness, anger, and chaos – in short, the Inner Warrior. In this woman's case, the fact that Mars is squaring many of her planets in Taurus cuts both ways – it provides more energy or directness than might otherwise be expected for so Venusian a temperament, while, at the same time, underscoring the potential difficulties of integrating that very same warrior energy. By her own admission, she experienced considerable challenges in dealing with anger and assertiveness earlier in her life, though in later years she has learned to deal with this conflict much more effectively.

Case History #3
Illustration 5 follows on the next page. Here we see the charts for actor and director Warren Beatty. As I noted before, one can tell a great deal about an individual's chakric make-up simply by looking to the position of their Sun and Moon. With Beatty's Sun in Aries and Moon in Scorpio, this chart shows a prominent emphasis on the "Inner Warrior." Indeed, Beatty has been known for his drive and competitiveness, both in and out of the movie industry. Early on, he gave up a possible career in sports (playing quarterback in collegiate football) to make his name and fortune as an actor and producer of numerous award-winning films. These capacities are effectively complemented by two planets in fourth-chakra Taurus (artistic and financial sensibility), and Jupiter in root-chakra Capricorn (political/business acumen and potential earth-plane success). Interestingly, his most personal and ambitious film was the lengthy and critically-acclaimed *Reds* about reporter-turned-political revolutionary, Jack Reed – the color red, of course, is commonly associated with Mars. As an actor, he won an early academy award playing a well-known gangster (or underworld warrior) in the film *Bonnie and Clyde*. Also worth calling attention to is his concurrent reputation as a jet-setting playboy, having courted and seduced a seemingly endless string of actresses and glamorous women from around the world. While the sexual drive is commonly associated with the second chakra, there is much to suggest that the third, or martian, chakra is also important in this respect (even the symbol for Mars resembles an erect phallus). I am repeatedly struck by how consistently a strong emphasis at this chakric level seems to indicate not only assertiveness, but an extraordinary, and sometimes even uncontrollable, libido as well.

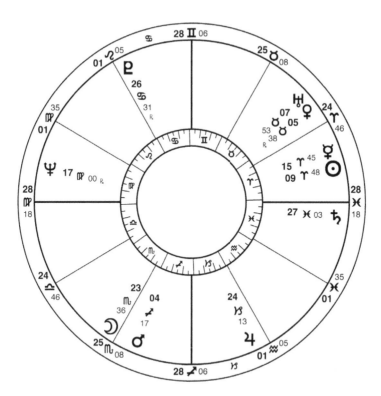

Illustration 5: Warren Beatty
March 30, 1937, 5:30 PM EST, Richmond, Virginia, USA

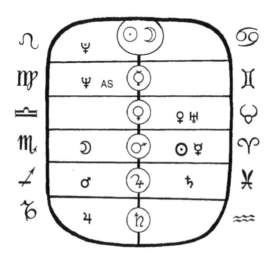

Illustration 6: Martin Luther
November 19, 1483, 11:00 PM LMT, Eiselben, Germany

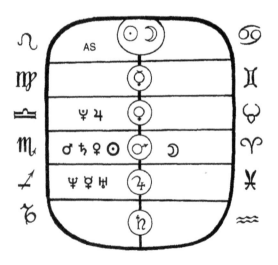

Case History #4

Illustration 6 depicts the chakric chart of Martin Luther, the man who single-handedly broke ranks with the reigning Catholic authorities during the 16th century, thereby initiating the Protestant reformation throughout Europe. Here is an example of a chart in which not one but two chakric levels are strongly emphasized and interconnected. In Luther's case, this involves the chakras specifically connected with what I have called the "Inner Warrior" and the "Inner Preacher" – the third and second chakras, respectively. Certainly, Luther combined these two energies through his highly persistent and combative efforts to establish a more independent religious sensibility for his time.

Case History #5

In illustration 7 (overleaf) we see an even more extraordinary convergence of energies, with no less than seven major indicators (not to mention the Ascendant) located in Aquarius alone. This indicates a strong emphasis on the first, or Saturn, chakra – but with an intriguing twist. In contrast to Capricorn, an earth sign on an earth chakra, Aquarius is an air sign transposed onto an earth chakra. Wherever we find air, the element of mentality, superimposed on the chakric ladder, we find the processes of mind applied to the unique concerns of that level. In Libra, for example, we see the air element transposed onto the heart chakra – hence, mentality is in service of more aesthetic or interpersonal concerns; Librans are therefore often associated with the arts and diplomacy. In Gemini, we find air applied to the throat chakra, in short, the most purely "platonic" form of mentality possible within the zodiac, with less concern for the practical applications of that knowledge. In Aquarius, however, we see the element of air applied to the earth chakra – hence the principle of mentality is in service to more physical-plane material concerns. It is therefore fitting that we see this sign (and its corresponding planet) so prominently emphasized in the charts of inventors, social reformers, scientists, and engineers. The person represented here is, in fact, an engineer, with far-ranging aspirations of changing the world through improved technology and living habitats.

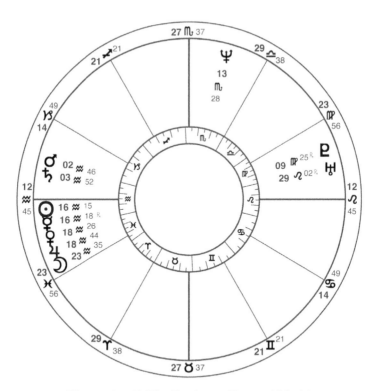

Illustration 7: The Engineer. Data withheld.

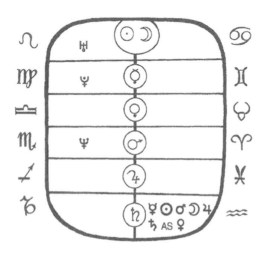

This, then, has been only the briefest introduction to yogic chakric philosophy, and some of the ways it can illuminate our understanding of the conventional, or Western horoscope. It is my hope that in the years to come a further exploration of this synthesis will provide us with the foundation for a true "sacred psychology" that more fully unlocks astrology's spiritual potentials.

Notes

1. Specifically, my thanks to Goswami Kriyananda (of Chicago) and Shelly Trimmer, a direct disciple of Paramahansa Yogananda, for first drawing my attention to this system of chakric-planetary correspondences. Importantly, this system is not exclusive to the Kriya Yoga tradition; one finds the same essential framework of correspondences described by such diverse writers as David Frawley (*Astrology of the Seers*), Jeff Green (*Uranus*), Titus Burckhardt (*Alchemy*), and Marc Edmund Jones (in his privately circulated "Sabian Assembly" lessons), derived in each case from largely independent sources.

2. Although the yogic tradition tends to discuss this subject in somewhat literal terms (e.g., karmic "seeds"), it is likely that karmas are not actually stored in specific points of space, but simply find their greatest degree of resonance within these chakric locations. By way of analogy, a diseased liver would not be regarded by a holistic healer as a problem only of the liver, but as a systemic condition that has its greatest focus in that bodily area – indeed, since the liver is associated by correspondence with the planet Jupiter, we might even say, astrologically, that the liver condition extends all the way out to involve Jupiter itself. Similarly, it is more accurate to say that karma is a field-phenomenon which extends through both space and time, on many different levels of consciousness simultaneously, but which resonates to certain nodal points in the chakric system in particularly concise ways.

Reprinted from *The Mountain Astrologer*, April 1996.

7

On the Perils of Telling People What to Do:
The Razor's Edge of Astrological Counseling

"Should I marry this person?"

"Is this job right for me?"

"What would be a good time for me to have plastic surgery?"

If your astrological practice is anything like mine, these are just a few of the questions you might receive from clients who come to you for insight into the workings of their lives. Years ago, I would have done my best to answer such questions and come up with some sort of definitive "yes" or "no" response. After all, these people were paying me for advice – weren't they?

But like the old Bob Dylan song goes, "Ah, but I was so much older then, I'm younger than that now..." Over the years I've found myself taking a more cautious – and hopefully subtler – approach toward my duties as an astrologer, as I've thought long and hard about what these duties really entail. Am I truly there to make up my clients' minds for them concerning significant life decisions? More importantly, perhaps, what are the real consequences – for both the client and myself – of saying things that could alter a person's life forever? As tempting as it may sometimes be to "help" a person through a genuinely difficult period, there is a thin line between truly helpful counsel and unwise interference with another person's destiny.

Here's one example of what I mean: Many years ago, a friend called to say he was going to travel with a tour group through China in a few months. He had never set foot outside the United States in his entire life, so he was eagerly looking forward to this opportunity and began preparing for his trip in every possible way. Just out of curiosity, and without telling him, I decided to check out his horoscope – and was somewhat startled to find a host of challenging transits firing in his horoscope precisely when he would be on this trip (specifically, powerful Pluto, Uranus, and Saturn transits and progressions). Yes, there was a decent Jupiter trine thrown in for good measure, not to mention a subtle Neptune sextile as well, but by and large it was the sort of astrological profile I myself would probably have avoided were I planning a trip by the stars.

What to do? Should I tell him about his decidedly mixed aspects or button my lip and keep it all to myself? A few years earlier, I would probably have done the "altruistic" thing by volunteering my advice on the matter, and thus sparing him the problems of a potentially terrible trip. But the day before drawing up his chart, it happened that I had stumbled across a passage in a spiritually-oriented book that impressed me deeply and set me to thinking. The passage stated that true mystics or gurus never volunteer their teaching uninvited – a spiritual version of Star Trek's "prime directive" of noninterference, you might say. I'd heard this general idea before, but because it popped up so close in time to this current dilemma, it made me reflect all the more deeply on my tendency to offer counsel to friends or family even when it wasn't beckoned. So after deliberating for a bit, I decided to hold off telling my friend what I thought about his difficult planetary energies during the upcoming trip to China.

So, what happened? As it turned out, my friend went on the trip – and it proved to be a life-changing experience in ways that neither of us could have foreseen. While he was hiking through a remote region of China with his tour group, a local villager in a nearby area suffered serious injuries; my friend knew some basic first aid, so he became closely involved with the rescue efforts. As could be expected under the transits, the entire scene was indeed one of chaos and anxiety, yet the resulting experience marked a key turning point in his young life. Not only did it bring him into contact with an aspect of foreign culture he wouldn't have experienced otherwise, but it also served as a catalyst for his becoming more involved with humanitarian activities on a global scale.

And most likely, none of this would have even happened had I opened my big fat mouth and volunteered my sage advice early on.

A Fine Line
Since then, I've been much more careful about freely, or at least too casually, dispensing my advice to people. But what if a client asks me for my advice on major life decisions? Surely that wouldn't violate the spiritual principle of noninterference, would it? But even then, I find myself being as careful and nondirective as humanly possible. After all, who among us is truly wise enough to know all the ramifications of any given situation, whether acted upon or not? No astrologer is omniscient. We cannot know all the variables of any situation, so we need to approach our discipline with a certain humility regarding our own grasp of "what is best" – or what isn't.

Even more to the point, who can say that a certain experience should be avoided simply because it may prove physically or emotionally difficult? How can we really know for sure what lessons a person might need to learn from a certain challenging situation? History is replete with individuals whose lives were changed – or whose lives, in turn, changed the world – by seemingly difficult experiences. Take Rosa Parks, the black woman who almost single-handedly initiated a civil rights revolution in the early 1960s by refusing to move to the back of that Birmingham bus. Without knowing her actual horoscope, it's safe to say that Ms. Parks probably had some very "challenging" aspects during the time of her epochal confrontation. I've sometimes wondered how I would have handled it had someone like that come to me for astrological counsel beforehand and asked me what to do during that particular period. Would I have told Rosa to simply avoid confrontational situations during that time? Or even stay at home on those "bad" days? Much as I hate to admit it, I fear that, 25 years ago, I probably would have done my best to steer such a person away from potentially difficult situations like those.

What is the solution here? Do we simply refrain entirely from giving advice or pointing the client in one direction or another? Not necessarily. There are some things that I would suggest as corrective measures when dealing with this problem:

First, I try to remember that my role as an astrological consultant is not to make up my clients' minds for them, nor to tell them how to live their lives; rather, it's to provide them with as much information as possible to best help them make their own decisions. In that respect, the astrologer is less of a guru than a coach – helping to draw out the client's own inner wisdom and intuition in situations.

Astrologer Christina Fielding remarked that she prefers to see the client as "driving the car," while she is the "ride-along," the person reading the map. In that spirit, I see my purpose as being there to help to illuminate the situation as fully as possible and to point out the potential ramifications of the situations or decisions to be encountered on the road ahead – while ultimately leaving the final decision up to my clients. As part of that ride-along process, I may choose to inform them as comprehensively as possible of both the "good" and "bad" possibilities inherent in any option before them, but I don't make the final judgment call.

Here's a simple example that illustrates how this might work. Say a predominantly Aries individual walks into my office and asks whether he should marry someone who, it turns out, is also a heavily Aries personality type. Taking a simplistic and judgmental approach, I might well look at this situation and tell him that two Aries-type individuals forming a partnership could make for a fairly volatile combination and, for that reason, might best be avoided. But taking a more nondirective, noncoercive approach, I could instead point out to the client the potential problems he could encounter along with the potential perks that could arise from such a synastry – and let him decide which way to go with it. Indeed, such volatility might prove to be the very thing that a given individual might want in a relationship. I once heard an astrology teacher say: "If you want to end a relationship with an Aries, simply stop arguing with them. They'll get bored and go search out someone else to do battle with!" A bit oversimplified, perhaps, but fairly accurate, based on my own field research. The key here is that I haven't told the client what to do, but merely helped to illumine his choices.

Now, let's consider how this same non-prescriptive approach might be applied in a more predictive setting, using transits or progressions. Take our earlier example of my friend's trip to China: Had my friend come to me before leaving on his trip and asked for my opinion of the energies at work during that time, I could have told him that the chart indeed indicated some challenging times ahead that might even involve a major crisis of some sort. But I would also have made it clear that this didn't necessarily mean he shouldn't go on the trip! Not only were there some Jupiter and Neptune trines and sextiles happening at the time, but I might have pointed out to him that the challenging aspects could make for a potentially transformative set of experiences which might be important to him.

But what if I saw no "harmonious" aspects to balance out the challenging energies at the time, and there was a real possibility of bodily danger or long-term problems arising from the trip? In those cases, I would make the client aware of the true extent of the difficulties, yet still be careful not to tell him what to do. For instance, my personal preference for handling such a situation would be to say something along these lines: "I can't tell you whether to go on this trip or not, but what I can say is what *I* would do if I were confronted by this set of energies – and in this case, I would personally choose not to travel under those transits." Period. By taking this approach, I have avoided making up the client's mind for him, and I have also avoided the potentially difficult karma of changing his life, one way or another – a factor that all astrologers should keep in mind when dispensing advice to friends or clients. What's critical here is that I have honestly given my assessment of the situation from an astrological standpoint – the very thing my clients pay me for – yet I have not compromised my own standards in the process.

Helping Clients Help Themselves
The other point I want to make is a bit more subtle but, in some ways, even more important: My job as a more esoterically-based consultant is to help clients to get in touch with their own reserves of intuition in situations and to draw upon those reserves when making their own decisions regarding these situations. A useful analogy here is the Chinese book of wisdom, the *I Ching*. This ancient text was never really intended by its creators to simply answer questions about major life decisions, but rather to provide a series of metaphorical images that could serve to unlock the individual's own inner wisdom regarding those problems. By reflecting on a symbol that arises in response to a question, one begins to understand the hidden dynamics underlying everyday situations.

What does all this mean on a practical level, when dealing with astrology clients? Let's say a person comes to me and asks whether she should pursue a certain career or not. After giving her all of the input I can, in terms of what the horoscope says about her life or hidden talents, I might ask her to stop for a moment and try to get in touch with what she feels. As Milton Erickson and therapists like him have long told us, there is profound wisdom contained within the unconscious, if we could but learn to tap into it. And one simple way of doing that is by slowing down the mind, as well as the breath.

Close your eyes, and notice how your body/mind feels when contemplating a decision. Does your stomach tighten up in anxiety when you consider this choice? Do you feel a certain "yes!" whispering from deep within when you contemplate that option? More often than not, I find that people already know at an intuitive level the right thing to do – they're just looking for an outside confirmation of that inner knowing.

This is how I've come to see my role as an astrologer in the lives of people who come to me for advice or insight. Of course, this stance isn't popular with every one of my clients, especially those who are looking for someone to take responsibility for their lives. But with each passing year, I'm convinced that this is the wisest approach both for them and myself. It leaves me with a clearer conscience about my impact on others' lives, and it helps me to maintain some semblance of dignity about my own role as an astrologer. After all, when I got into astrology some 30 years ago and was first enraptured by the possibilities of a life immersed in the wisdom of the stars, somehow that vision didn't include the prospect of telling people the best times for plastic surgery, or whether to marry that Elvis impersonator from Dubuque.

Reprinted from *The Mountain Astrologer*, October/November 2001.

8

Astrology Goes to the Movies:
Exploring Planetary Symbolism in the Cinema

For most people, going to the movies is just an opportunity to escape from the concerns and responsibilities of everyday life, a few minutes when we can step into an imaginary world of excitement and fantasy. But for astrologers, the cinema also offers a virtual motherlode of symbolism that often sheds light on the shifting planetary patterns of the time. For several decades now, I've watched in fascination as astrological configurations reflect themselves in the images and stories of popular movies, whether those be serious "art" films or the most commercial and populist of entertainments. On its surface, for instance, a movie might have the trappings of an ordinary adventure tale; yet peer just beneath the surface and you might be surprised to find a play of archetypal energies that describes a mythic drama being mirrored in the stars right at that time. In this article I'd like to explore a few examples of this.

Uranus in Pisces and *The Da Vinci Code*

As a simple illustration, consider the passage of the outer planets through the zodiacal signs, and how this might reflect itself in the global zeitgeist. Astrologers especially regard the planetary bodies out beyond Saturn as "generational" indicators in the way they tend to relate to broader, transpersonal trends taking place throughout the world. When Uranus moved into Pisces in 2003, for example, we started to witness a growing surge of interest around the world in that most Piscean of religions, Christianity – its origins, beliefs, political influence, moral precepts, and so on. As one market analyst remarked on TV interview at the time, "Christianity has suddenly become big business."

Among the cinematic expressions of that shift was Mel Gibson's unlikely blockbuster *Passion of the Christ* (which premiered precisely as a solar eclipse underscored Uranus' position in Pisces), as well as *The Chronicles of Narnia*, a film adaptation of C.S. Lewis' thinly disguised re-telling of the Christ story. But as might be expected with this rebellious planet, there were also books, TV shows, and films that challenged longstanding views of Christianity. These included the publication of the long-lost *Gospel of Judas*, which not only upended our conventional views of this much maligned figure but pointed out how deeply astrological ideas suffused early Christianity.

Though by far the most controversial reframing of Christian beliefs came in the form of Dan Brown's hugely successful book, and subsequent film, *The Da Vinci Code*. In addition to challenging longstanding assumptions about the role of Mary Magdalene in early Christianity, Brown interspersed a host of other controversial or "new age" ideas in his discussion, including the church's suppression of women, the role of the zodiacal "Great Ages," and the mystical dimension of Christ's spiritual teachings, among others. For the vast majority of mainstream churchgoers, these were surprising, possibly even heretical ideas; but for astrologers, they seemed a fitting expression of the turbulent effects of Uranus moving through the spiritual sign of Pisces.

The Voyager II Fly-by to Neptune

Sometimes, the synchronicities between the planetary aspects and films arise in unexpected ways. For instance, in 1989 NASA's unmanned Voyager II spacecraft made its scheduled fly-by past the distant planet Neptune, providing us with our first close-up look at this mysterious body. It was at that point that we were treated to a litany of new stories that symbolically expressed both the constructive and destructive influences of this celestial body.

Reflecting the darker side of Neptune, that included news accounts of an unprecented surge in the drug war which climaxed in an epidemic of drug-related violence in Central and South America – including Columbian drug lords openly declaring war on their own government. Concerns over the festering situation became so grave that, north of the border, president George Bush Sr. scheduled an impromptu talk on nationwide TV to discuss it with the American public, which coincided almost exactly with the closest approach of the Voyager spacecraft to Neptune.

Cinematically, though, perhaps the clearest expressions of this rising Neptunian energy was a spate of films throughout that year centering on oceanic and watery themes: *Deepstar Six, Leviathan, The Navigator,* and most conspicuous of all, James Cameron's *The Abyss*. Appropriate for oceanic Neptune, this visually striking film was set largely underwater and concerned an attempt by scientists to grapple with a life-threatening problem involving nuclear materials lodged deep undersea. The movie concluded with a haunting sequence in which the central character (played by Ed Harris) performs the ultimate Neptunian act by offering to sacrifice his life for the sake of the world, plunging thousands of feet down to the ocean's bottom. At the last possible moment, he is rescued by highly advanced extraterrestrial beings who are living in a base they've constructed deep down on the sea bed

Planetary Patterns on the Silver Screen
Another way that astrological symbolism often feeds into popular films is in connection with the dominant planetary configurations of the day. When spacious Jupiter aligned with idealistic Neptune in Aquarius back in 2009, for example, one expression of that synergy was the popular Pixar film *Up!* Employing state-of-the-art computer graphics, it portrayed an elderly man's wildly expansive dreams of escaping to a far-off land by means of multi-colored balloons attached to his house. The elements of ascension, escape, and gaseousness all concisely reflected the qualities of both these planets in tandem, as did the aviation-oriented sign of Aquarius these bodies were transiting through at the time.

To my mind, one of the most dramatic planetary combinations to reflect itself in the films of a period is when Uranus moves into stressful aspect with Saturn – the proverbial "odd couple" of the solar system. For instance, two of the most critically acclaimed films of 1999 were *American Beauty* and David Fincher's violent masterwork *Fight Club*. Released within just weeks of each other, these two films featured a number of uncanny parallels, such as: both involved stories of middle-age men striving to break free of suffocating, conventional environments in order to experience freer, more uninhibited lifestyles; both films depict their lead character being spurred into action by the inspiration of wilder, more free-spirited mentors; both movies feature strikingly similar scenes where the central character "sticks it to the system" by extorting large amounts of money from an oppressive employer (in both cases by means of ungrounded, scandalous accusations); and both films conclude with their lead characters taking a bullet in the head just as they finally attain "peace of mind" – of a sort.

Not too surprisingly, the dominant astrological pattern of that period was conventional Saturn in Taurus squaring unconventional Uranus in Aquarius. The tension between the two lead characters in both movies acted out this planetary configuration to perfection. But as with all such instances, it's important to remember that cinematic synchronicities like these actually reflect a struggle taking place in all our personal lives as well. In this case, the square from Uranus was likely pointing to fundamental changes taking place with our own inner "Saturns" at that time – i.e., our accepted perspectives and attitudes towards tradition, authority, and society. In the lives of my clients and friends during that time, for instance, I noticed major changes and challenges coming to the fore in ways that echoed those of these cinematic characters in surprisingly similar ways.

Citizen Kane and the Great Taurus Line-up

Of all the configurations I've studied in connection with cinematic trends, one in particular stands out for me, due to the unique blend of planetary and zodiacal influences it embodies. I'm referring to the epic alignment of planets that climaxed between late April and early May of 1941.

What makes this period so special? To begin with, throughout the late 1930s and early 1940s Uranus was entangled in a creative trine with Neptune, a combination partly responsible for the impressive run of classic films released during those same years: *Casablanca*, *Gone with the Wind*, *The Wizard of Oz*, and *The Grapes of Wrath*, among many others. Also worth noting is the slew of popular performers born during that same period who went on to electrify the 1960s, including John Lennon, Jimi Hendrix, Joni Mitchell, Paul McCartney, Brian Wilson, and Mick Jagger.

While that trine between Uranus and Neptune completed exactly at several points during that entire period, it arguably reached its climax between April 30 and May 8 of 1941. That's when a series of other planetary configurations came together as well, reinforcing the power of that trine many times over. During that roughly one week-long window, Jupiter entered the picture and conjoined Uranus while simultaneously trining Neptune, making for a cosmic trifecta of Jupiter conjunct Uranus, Jupiter trine Neptune, and Uranus trine Neptune – all at the exact same time! And as we'll explore in more detail later in this volume, that three-fold pattern unfolded in the context of a powerful multi-planet lineup in Taurus, which included such other planetary aspects as Saturn conjunct Jupiter, and Saturn conjunct Venus, and Saturn conjunct Uranus! Taken all together, this was a planetary and zodiacal period like few others in recent history.

As it so happened, that window of time saw the release of a film many critics have since dubbed "the greatest ever made"– *Citizen Kane.* Premiering in New York on May 1, 1941, Orson Welles' tour de force daringly told the story of a wealthy media mogul from multiple perspectives, employing technical innovations and a nonlinear storyline that prefigured the later movies of directors like Quentin Tarantino, Robert Altman, and Stanley Kubrick. Considering the Taurus emphasis in effect during the film's release, there's something fitting about the fact that a primary theme of the movie is that of materialism; indeed, the movie's lead character is depicted as having been adopted at a young age by a bank! But reflecting the more aesthetic side of Taurus, Welles' movie also features many strikingly beautiful moments. Here is what critic Jesse Zunser had to say in the now-defunct *Cue* magazine, employing some surprisingly Taurean nature-metaphors to do so:

> You come away limp, much as if you had turned into Broadway and suddenly beheld Niagara Falls towering behind the Paramount Building, the Matterhorn looming over Bryant Park, and the Grand Canyon yawning down the middle of Times Square.

A side note about planetary cycles: at the time I began writing about *Citizen Kane* in 1999, I started noticing a number of other references to Welles in various media sources. For instance, HBO premiered its made-for-TV film on the making of *Citizen Kane*, titled *RKO 281*, and not long after that, Tim Robbins' film about Orson Welles, *Cradle Will Rock*, made its way into theaters. 1999 was also when United States Post Office released a 1940s' commemorative stamp featuring Orson Welles in the role of Charles Foster Kane on it.

I wondered what accounted for this sudden surge of Wellesmania. Turning to Welles' birth chart, I discovered that he was undergoing his Uranus return exactly as all these developments were taking place. By this point, however, Welles had been dead for some 15 years! But as I mentioned in chapter 1, one of astrology's true peculiarities is the vexing fact that horoscopes continue to live on long after their owners do!

In other words, media events sometimes reflect activations of horoscopes from long before. That's true not only for people, incidentally, but for historic events. For instance, James Cameron's film *Titanic* appeared 84 years after the tragedy itself, bringing that historic event back into the world's consciousness in dramatic fashion. In a similar manner, Fritz Lang's 1927 film *Metropolis* was a box-office flop when it first appeared, but slowly developed an audience among film fans through the decades. Shortly after its release, its running time was severely cut by both the studio and distributors, so that what audiences saw was only a pale shadow of Lang's original work. But to the delight (and surprise) of many, much of the original missing footage turned up in South America and a restored version of the film was finally re-released on the movie's Uranus return, in 2009.

These, then, are just a few examples of how films can express the shifting energies of the zeitgeist. The next time you go the movies, perhaps take a few moments afterwards to consider how the story and its symbols might shed light on the dominant planetary patterns of the time. There are many ways to learn about astrology and its influence in our world, including even the stories we enjoy up on the silver screen.

Reprinted from *Dell Horoscope*, November 2012.

9

The Dawn of Aquarius
The Turning of the Great Ages

Imagine the world as it might appear from the perspective of an ant wandering on-stage during a performance of Shakespeare's *A Midsummer Night's Dream*. All around you there unfolds a great drama, replete with exotic colors, sounds, and complex happenings; yet because of your limited perspective, the meaning of it all escapes you. You can't comprehend the multi-layered significance of this drama, nor grasp how these diverse elements fit into the greater unfolding narrative being played out over several acts. Only by understanding that larger context can you truly see how those transitory events are integral facets of a broader pattern of meaning, a greater story.

In a way, our own predicament is rather like that. We, too, find ourselves meandering across a great "stage" – that of history itself. To the casual eye, the events transpiring around us may seem like a chaotic jumble of random occurrences: a rocket carrying seven crew members explodes in mid-air; a world leader finds himself embroiled in a foreign war; a new computer technology suddenly takes the world by storm. At first glance there is little to suggest such things possess any meaning or relation to one another. Yet our problem may simply be one of proximity: perhaps we are simply too close to grasp what is going on. If only our perspectives were broad enough, perhaps we could recognize how these isolated events were actually facets of a much larger story.

For the esotericist, an important key toward helping unlock that broader perspective lies in a concept known as the *Great Ages*. We presently find ourselves straddling the threshold between "acts," as it were, between the Piscean and the Aquarian Ages. Like vast tectonic plates shifting deep within the collective unconscious, this epochal transition has already begun manifesting as a series of seismic changes throughout our world, as the forms of an older order make way for those of a radically new one. Will the coming era be a time of "peace, love, and brotherhood," as some suggest? Or will it instead bring about an Orwellian police state where men and women are little more than cogs in a bureaucratic machine? As always, the truth will almost certainly be more complex than we expect, or perhaps even imagine. It's useful to remember that the same Piscean Age which brought us Jesus Christ also brought us Torquemada and the Inquisition, not to mention evangelist Jimmy Swaggert. To help us make sense of these unfolding complexities, let us look briefly at a few of the key symbols and archetypal themes associated with both of these shifting eras.

The Age of Pisces (c. 1 A.D. to 2100 A.D.)

For two millennia now, we have been under the influence primarily of the watery sign of Pisces. Among the manifestations of the Piscean Age has been the rise of a global religion centering primarily on symbols of water: baptism, walking on water, changing water into wine, and so forth. Indeed, for the student of astrological symbolism Christianity offers a virtual mother lode of correspondences in connection with Pisces. For example, Christian scripture speaks extensively of fishermen, sympathy for society's outcasts, martyrdom, and the washing of feet – all traditional symbols of Pisces. One of the defining miracles of Christ's ministry was the feeding of the multitude with two fishes and five loaves of bread. More subtly, the eating of fish on Friday by Catholics is linked by some to the fact that Friday is governed by Venus, the planet that is "exalted" (i.e., attains its optimal expression) in Pisces.

Were such correspondences intentional on the part of the Church fathers, or was their emergence purely synchronistic? Even scholars disagree on this point, so we may never know for sure. But either way we can study these symbols for what they reveal about the archetypal dynamics of the time. Viewed as a whole, they tell us that humanity was learning to relate to reality and the divine through a more emotional filter. In its constructive aspect, this brought about a newfound element of compassion and faith in key segments of society, especially within the Christian world. Anaimal sacrifice was abandoned, and there arose a spiritual sensibility that spoke of "turning the other cheek" rather than the smiting of enemies. It was a shift from *Roma* to *Amor*, one could say.

In a more negative vein, this same emphasis on emotionality ushered in a spirit of dogmatism and persecution within the emerging religions. Pisces is intensely concerned with matters of faith, but taken to extremes this can lead to zealotry, self-righteousness, and the urge to establish absolute guidelines for all to follow. At its worst, the Piscean Age was an era of religious intolerance, when large populations were expected to show unquestioning allegiance to a monolithic belief system, as exhibited in much of Christianity and Islam during this time.

One of the more striking Piscean symbols found in Christianity is its central image: the crucifixion. It is sobering to consider that for nearly two thousand years Western culture has defined itself largely in terms of an image of a man nailed to a cross, tortured in a most gruesome manner. Yet viewed archetypally, this singular seed-image contains the best and worst of the Piscean legacy. On a negative level, the crucifixion expresses dark Piscean qualities like self-pity, masochism, guilt, and martyrdom. These traits reflect the ego-dissolving principle of water but directed in a more destructive, self-abnegating way. In some respects the Piscean Age might well be called the ultimate age of neurosis, this being an era when many felt that suffering and guilt were somehow synonymous with spirituality. This is precisely the sort of delusion that arises when the ego is unhealthy or ungrounded, and finds itself drawn back into the more corrosive and self-destructive emotions of the soul.

But the crucifixion has a more positive interpretation, too. As astrologers know, Pisces symbolically relates to the transcendence of the ego and the surrendering of personal interests in service of a higher ideal. As the last sign in the zodiac (determined by the sun's counter-clockwise movement), Pisces is that final stage in the soul's evolution where the boundaries of personality have begun to dissolve and the soul now merges with the cosmic ocean of existence. This is what the crucifixion means in its highest sense: the willing capacity for sacrifice, worship, and profound devotion. This is the water element at its most refined. Some examples of this higher aspect of Pisces would be St. Francis of Assisi, or the ideals of chivalry and courtly love, with their ethos of self-sacrifice and idealism, that arose during the medieval era. Note, too, that the word for that other major Piscean Age religion, Islam, means "surrender" when translated into English.

Whereas the Age of Aries brought an awakening of the outwardly-directed ego, the more feminine Piscean Age brought about a newfound sense of interiority or inwardness. In religious terms, this was evident in the emerging Christian emphasis on moral reflectivity, or conscience. The flip side of this development, unfortunately, was the emergence of a new mood of guilt throughout Western society. Prior to Christianity, one rarely finds a sense of conscience or "sin" as we now think of it. By way of contrast, the earlier Greeks saw their relationship to the gods in more mechanical and external terms than we do now. When crimes were committed, one atoned for them not because of an inner sense of guilt so much as a belief that one had accrued a "stain" of sorts which could be removed through an appropriate sacrifice.

On another level, this new sense of interiority was mirrored in the rise of architectural features like the dome and the arch, so critical to the Islamic mosque or Roman structures like the Pantheon. This interiority was visible as well as in the introduction of pupils into the eyes of Roman statues early in the Age; examine the ancient busts of early Romans and the Greeks and one finds that their eyes have no pupils. Artistic shifts like these symbolized a new world of emotions opening up during the early Christian era. It was a development that, centuries later, made possible the later birth of modern psychology.

The Age of Aquarius (c. 2100 A.D. to 4200 A.D.)

The most frequently asked question concerning the Aquarian Age is, *when* does it begin? That is a bit like determining when the dawn starts. Is it when the morning sky first starts glowing, long before the actual sunrise? Or is it when the sun actually appears over the horizon?

The same problem applies to understanding the timing of the Great Ages. An Age doesn't begin on a single day or year, but unfolds gradually over many years, exerting its influence in pronounced waves like an incoming tide. Consequently while the Aquarian Age may not fully manifest for several centuries yet (most estimates suggest somewhere between 2100 and 2800 A.D.), there are many examples to suggest its symbols are already appearing in our world. The internet and democracy are but two expressions of this.

Whereas Pisces is traditionally associated with the element of water, Aquarius is associated with air. Exoterically, this is reflected in the startling rise of aviation technologies and space travel over the last two centuries. Humans are quite literally learning to master the air realm, not only through aviation but in the construction of ever-taller buildings that allow us to live higher up off the ground. The media also employs metaphors which reflect this elemental shift when it says that a show goes "on the air," or when a broadcaster "takes to the airwaves."

Such outer developments are only reflections of an inner shift taking place throughout the culture, one that relates to an awakening of *mind* in human evolution. Understood symbolically, air is the medium through which we communicate our thoughts and ideas, and is the element most associated with rationality and thinking. What this means is that the Aquarian Age will undoubtedly witness advances in humanity's intellectual growth, no doubt at widely varying levels of sophistication. Someone living life in front of their TV set can be said to be pursuing a "mental" existence, but one quite different in quality from that of a scientist struggling to unlock the mysteries of the cosmos. Terms like "information superhighway" or the "information revolution" are further examples of how the impending Aquarian influence has already begun to propel our world toward more mental values and modes of experience. The modern separation of church and state is another important example of the disengaging of our rational minds from the dogmatic and emotional concerns of the Piscean Age.

A vital key toward understanding the meaning of Aquarius resides in the way each of the different elements repeats itself three times over the course of the zodiac. In other words, there are three earth signs, three water signs, three fire signs, and three air signs. With each version of that element, we find that elemental principle expressing itself in subtly different ways. To illustrate this, let us focus here on the trio of air signs: Gemini, Libra, and Aquarius.

The Three Faces of Air
Given the progressive nature of the zodiac, it is not surprising that each of these three signs might reflect the workings of the mind in broader and more impersonal ways. For instance, in Gemini, rationality expresses itself in highly personal ways: through the workings of the everyday mind and through ordinary forms of communication. In Libra, the rationality of the air element manifests in a more interpersonal way, through a mentality directed toward interactions with others in wider social contexts. An example of this would be a teacher standing before a class, or a salesman dealing with clients.

In Aquarius, we find the element of air-rationality expressing itself through the most impersonal contexts of all – in terms of the masses, or even the cosmos itself. Aquarius could be described as the principle of cosmic rationality or cosmic mind, the ability to perceive and make connections of the most abstract and cosmic sort. Aquarius isn't simply concerned with ideas and theoretical relations; it is concerned with ideas and relationships that are global or universal in scope.

For this reason, the Aquarian Age will likely be an era when science, rather than religion, will be the dominant paradigm, and its scientists the new high priests. Rather than focus its attention on any one individual's ideas or feelings, science attempts to uncover laws and principles that apply everywhere, and everywhen. This same impersonality is also evident in the way many of us now are involved with social connections and networks extending over vast distances, through technologies like the internet or TV. These allow people across the world to communicate with one another, but in more cerebral ways. It is one of the paradoxes of our time that we find ourselves becoming more interconnected with people across the entire world while knowing less and less about the person living next door.

This shifting orientation toward Aquarian air is also responsible for the growing fascination we see with outer space and its exploration, as reflected in films like *Star Wars* or *2001: A Space Odyssey*, or TV shows like *Star Trek*. Works like these capture the emerging spirit of a "longing for the stars" that is so intrinsic to Aquarius. The modern fascination with UFOs and extraterrestrial life will likely become even more pronounced in the years to come, as humanity finds its speculations and fantasies in these areas transforming into hard reality.

Transitional Symbols on the Brink of Aquarius

With one foot in the Piscean Age behind us and the other in the Aquarian Age before us, we find ourselves caught between radically contrasting, and sometimes conflicting, value systems. If the Great Ages represent a Shakespearean drama of cosmic proportions, we have stepped onstage precisely at the point "between acts," as it were, when the old props and backdrops are being replaced by new ones. One result of living in this liminal or in-between state is the rise of various transitional forms – symbolic hybrids of Piscean and Aquarian energies together. Here are a few examples of these from recent times.

Televangelism: What happens when old-style Piscean Christianity meets up with Aquarian-style media technology? One result is that distinctly modern phenomenon called televangelism, where preachers employ the fruits of global technology for spreading the gospel of salvation to even larger audiences than before.

The Abortion Debate: As one age comes up against another, there can be a violent clashing of values and ideologies from both sides of the divide. A vivid example of this is the modern controversy over abortion. On the one hand we have the largely Christian-based "pro-life" advocates representing the values of the Piscean Age, reflecting sympathy for the helpless unborn. On the other hand there are the "pro-choice" advocates representing the forces of Aquarius, championing the rights of individuals to decide their own fates. Through the years there has been little compromise between these two camps, and there is little hope for change in sight, but with good reason. They arise out of two fundamentally different paradigms, two radically different ways of seeing and evaluating the world – one from the last Great Age and the other from the next.

The Storming of the Bastille: Even single events from history can sometimes serve as symbolic benchmarks in the transition between eras. One of the earliest and most dramatic examples of this was the storming of the Bastille on July 14, 1789, a pivotal event in the French Revolution. On this date, French radicals overtook and opened up the famed prison which had been holding political prisoners, and released those few who remained. In astrological symbolism, prisons are associated with Pisces, while the principles of freedom and revolution are associated with Aquarius. The opening up of a prison and release of its prisoners was a symbolic landmark in the move from the old authoritarian order to a more freedom-oriented one.

Alcoholics Anonymous: For astrologers, one of the negative symbols associated with Pisces has long been the addiction to intoxicants like alcohol, drugs, or even fossil fuel! Groups like Alcoholics Anonymous offer an example of people coming together to break free from their addiction to alcohol, nicely symbolizing the effort to undo our bondage to Piscean-Age consciousness. AA is thus a complex phenomenon: on the one hand, it has one foot firmly planted in the values of the receding age, as evidenced by its emphasis on surrendering to a higher power ("Let go and let God!"), as well as its own brand of "commandments" (the "twelve steps"). At the same time, AA is essentially democratic and non-denominational, qualities associated with the emerging era. Viewed archetypally, AA is a hybrid creation that blends the values of both Piscean and Aquarian Ages.

Transitional Symbols in Literature: The transition to the Aquarian Age has expressed itself within the forms of modern literature as well. For instance, the passage from one age to another sometimes expresses itself mythically in symbols which depict a hero doing battle with a creature associated with the prior age. A historical example from Western religion would be Moses casting out the golden calf, symbolizing the transition from the Age of Taurus to that of Aries.

In modern times, a similar pattern expresses itself in books like *Moby Dick*. In Herman Melville's sprawling novel we see a figure in the open air (Ahab) attempting to slay a creature of the sea, symbolizing transcendence over the water realm (Pisces). Additionally, if the whaling industry is taken as a symbol for modern industrial civilization generally (it was the first true industry to emerge from the young America), then Melville's tale underscores the shift from a more emotional age to the more technological and business-minded one of Aquarius.

On another level, it's possible to view Melville's tale as foreshadowing the cataclysm that was about to shake America to its core one decade later – the Civil War. Here, too, we saw a clash between Ages being acted out, with the Union forces, symbolizing the values of freedom (led by Abraham Lincoln – an Aquarian born on the same day as Charles Darwin), seeking to overturn the slavery-based world of the U.S. South.

Although very different on its surface, the same essential dynamic was at work more than a century later in the tragic story of government agents attacking David Koresh's religious compound in Waco, Texas. Whatever one's own thoughts about the attack or its possible justification, the symbolism is clear: a secular government imposing limits on a religious community – i.e., Aquarius restricting Pisces. The fact that the attack took place precisely as the planetary rulers of Aquarius and Pisces moved into alignment, when Uranus conjoined Neptune in 1993, succinctly underscores the archetypal meaning of the event.

The Pilgrims' Immigration to America: Whether we know it or not, we are all pushed or pulled to one degree or another by the imperatives of our age, we all act out the necessities of a broader drama. As a case in point, the attempt by pilgrims to flee religious persecution in the old world to find religious freedom in the new one reflected a shift from the more dogmatic and persecution-oriented Piscean era to the freedom-oriented Aquarian Age. Little could they have realized how they were also setting the stage for a collective drama whose implications would extend far into the future and influence the geopolitical direction of an entire planet for centuries to come.

Reprinted from *The Quest* magazine, Winter 2010, and *New Dawn Magazine*, May/June 2006.

10

Cinema and the Birth of the Aquarian Age

In various articles and books over the years, I've explored the way movies mirror global planetary trends at the time of their release, along with how they reflect the horoscopes of their directors. In this article, we will consider the possibility that films sometimes reflect even broader trends – including those associated with the shifting Great Ages. I'll reprise some selected ideas drawn from my book, *Signs of the Times*, along with material not included there, to demonstrate how the shift from Pisces to Aquarius may already be expressing itself, in both subtle and obvious ways, within in the imagery of modern films. It should become apparent that examples like these not only help us to better understand the transformation sweeping our world, but also deepen our insight into the underlying astrological principles themselves.

The Wizard of Oz
This 1939 film features one of the most enduringly popular tales of modern culture. Yet it also holds an important key for understanding the shift of consciousness we call the Aquarian Age. In L. Frank Baum's story, our four protagonists (Dorothy, the Cowardly Lion, the Tin Man, and the Scarecrow) set out on a great mission: One is looking for courage, another for brains, another for heart, and another simply wants to return home. The four travel together to Oz to meet the great and powerful wizard who sends them on a journey full of difficult trials, as prerequisites for attaining their dreams. Upon completing their tasks, however, they experience a great disillusionment, for they discover that the "great and powerful" wizard is nothing of the sort: He is simply an ordinary man. They learn that what they really seek lies somewhere much closer to home. "The answer has always been within you," Glynda the Good Witch tells Dorothy.

In this timeless tale, we see a beautiful expression of the seismic shift taking place in the unfolding of our spiritual sensibilities, as we move from a Piscean era when the answers were seen as largely residing outside of ourselves – in the form of gurus, priests, or God-like figures of one sort or another – to an Aquarian era when the Divine is seen within each of us. "Pay no attention to that man behind the curtain!" the wizard yells out, as our four seekers discover that the God-like figure is nothing but a sham. In a similar way, we are realizing now that the old institutions and God symbols have lost much of their currency. This echoes the German philosopher Nietzsche who, more than a century ago, declared that God is dead. That idea was never intended to address God's objective existence as much as our outworn conceptions of God. Likewise, *The Wizard of Oz* isn't suggesting that there is no Divinity but merely that we must rethink our approach to it. Our spirituality must be rooted in a personal experience that looks within for "salvation," rather than without. In other words, we are not the servants of God, but co-creators with God – a shift from Piscean dependency to Aquarian autonomy.

Did Baum himself intend these more esoteric implications with his seeming child's tale? It's fairly safe to say that he did, since Baum (born with Sun conjunct Uranus) had been a member of the Theosophical Society since 1892 and even wrote publicly about theosophical concepts for a South Dakota newspaper, the *Aberdeen Saturday Pioneer*. Among the central tenets of theosophy is the belief that Divinity resides inside us, rather than in any external form or intermediary. As Madame Blavatsky herself once phrased it, the essence of spiritual esotericism can be summed up as the concept that "the personal God exists within, nowhere outside, the worshipper."[1]

The Truman Show
In this ingenious 1998 film, directed by Peter Weir and scripted by Andrew Niccol, the lead character, Truman Burbank, is depicted as the star (or victim?) of a mass media show that he doesn't realize he's part of. Every move Truman makes is carefully captured by a constellation of TV cameras and broadcast to a worldwide audience who follows his daily life as though it were a soap opera. Over the course of the film, he gradually awakens to the nature of his predicament and struggles to break out of this media-saturated reality in order to forge his own life, free from the domination of the God-like powers manipulating his world.

On one level, this story speaks to the potential dangers we all face as our lives become increasingly entwined with surveillance cameras and information-gathering systems of every stripe. This could easily be one of the downsides of the information-oriented Aquarian Age; individual lives are scrutinized by technologies such as these, and personal privacy becomes an increasingly scarce commodity.

But Weir and Niccol's story touches on a much deeper level of resonance for any student of the Great Ages. The protagonist's struggle to awaken into freedom involves an effort to break free from a world bounded by water (Pisces) into one of air (Aquarius). Specifically, Truman must overcome his paralyzing fear of water. Each time he attempts to escape his world, he is enticed back by alcohol (Pisces, in its negative aspect). In the movie's closing sequence, he finally overcomes that fear and is shown literally stepping into the sky, ostensibly to begin his new life. (Note that in the original *Matrix*, Neo's awakening is also depicted as an escape from a water-based existence into an air-based one, when he emerges from the embryonic "pod" which has contained him since birth.)

Further underscoring this symbolism is the fact that the God-like "creator" who controlls Truman's world is named "Christof" — *of Christ*, as it were – a telling reference to the Piscean-Age religion bearing that figure's name. In short, Truman's efforts to break free of Christof's grip reflect our own collective struggle to throw off the lingering influence of the Piscean Age and its comparatively dogmatic mind-set, to pursue a more independent lifestyle. (Also note that in the film's production script, Christof's boss is named Moses, a reference to a key luminary of the previous Great Age, Aries!) In that respect, this film's message is vaguely similar to that of *The Wizard of Oz*: Truman must leave behind the external "God" symbols of his world to become a fully authentic person, or *true man* – an Aquarian revelation of the highest order.

Titanic

James Cameron's mega-blockbuster from 1997 centers around the ill-fated maiden voyage of the famed oceanliner as it made its way from Europe to a disastrous collision with an iceberg in the north Atlantic. At the emotional core of the story lies the tale of an ill-fated love affair between two young passengers on this ship, played by Leonardo DiCaprio and Kate Winslet.

As some commentators have pointed out over the years, the dominant thread in this story is really Rose's journey of awakening and survival. Over the course of her journey, we see a dramatic transformation in her character from the comparatively rigid values associated with her "old world" background, to the more liberated values associated with American society, as represented by Leo DiCaprio's character, Jack. At film's end, we glimpse photographs near Rose's deathbed that reveal she has lived a life inspired by ideals of freedom and self-determination – the very qualities associated with the Aquarian Age in its higher aspects. Further underscoring this theme is the way Leonardo DiCaprio's character is shown to completely bypass the established norms of where passengers are supposed to reside on this ship; while booked in lower-class sleeping quarters, he freely moves between decks, even mingling at one point with wealthy passengers in the first class dining room. In so doing, he expresses the more democratic and comparatively classless ideals of America, and in turn, Aquarian society.

Chocolat

Due to the principle of polarity, each Great Age emphasizes not only the sign normally associated with it, but also the sign opposite it. The Piscean Age, for example, emphasized both Pisces and Virgo – a zodiacal axis that, as anyone with these signs amplified in their chart knows, can lean toward a more dutiful and pleasure-denying approach to life. Over the last two millennia, this gave rise to (among other things) a world religion championing the virtues of austerity and sacrifice, as embodied in the grim image of a man hanging on a wooden cross. During this age, people commonly believed that there was something inherently virtuous in suffering itself and that it was somehow unspiritual to experience pleasure. In Islam, too, we see the spirit of abstinence regarding sex and alcohol – but qualified by the promise of great pleasures in the afterlife!

In the Aquarius/Leo Age, we can expect a vastly different value system, where the pursuit of personal pleasure is not only acceptable, it could even become an end in itself. That tectonic shift of archetypal values is nicely portrayed in Lasse Hallström's 2000 film, *Chocolat*. The movie is set in the 1950s, in a conservative Christian town in France, where all forms of personal pleasure and independent thought are strongly discouraged by the local church authorities. That worldview is suddenly challenged when a free-thinking woman comes to town, opens a gourmet chocolate shop, and manages to tempt these long-repressed citizens with her delectable offerings. Adding to the community's anger is this woman's blithe refusal to join the local church; instead, she opts to live more independently. The situation reaches a climax when she begins to fraternize with a group of long-haired vagabonds, "proto-hippies" of that time, who arrive by barge down a nearby river and whose liberal ways are even more threatening to local sensibilities. When the two worldviews finally clash, tragedy results – though, in the process, the community becomes transformed and awakened to a new world of personal pleasure.

The rigidly dogmatic and self-denying values advocated by the local Christian church in this film perfectly embody the negative aspects of the Piscean Age; the woman and her bohemian associates reflect the more life-affirming, liberal sensibilities of the Aquarius/Leo Age coming into play, so to speak. The collision of worldviews in this movie reflects a very real clash of values that has been gaining momentum for several centuries now – as spearheaded by such real-world figures as Lord Byron, Jean Jacques Rousseau, and the latter-day hippies, all of whom point the way to a more pleasure-oriented approach to life. This film shows us the more positive side of this trend; for the other side of the coin, let us turn now to our next film.

The Sound of Music
Another example of that tension between adjoining Ages can be found in Robert Wise's film version of the Broadway musical, *The Sound of Music*. The most successful movie of its time, it premiered in 1965 – the same year as the first Uranus/Pluto conjunction which shaped that decade. I put off seeing it for years since I mistakenly assumed it was little more than light entertainment with no further value for me as an esotericist. So imagine my surprise when I finally caught up with it and discovered how the film's core narrative reflected the shift from Pisces to Aquarius in a fairly dramatic way!

Consider the film's central story of a young woman named Maria (played by Julie Andrews) who lives in a Catholic convent and aspires to be a nun. As the plot unfolds, she finds herself attracted to the patriarch of a local musical family she's been called on to tutor, a Captain Georg von Trapp (played by Christopher Plummer). They eventually fall in love, and after much soul-searching, she decides to leave her life of religious service behind in order to pursue a life of romantic happiness in marriage. Viewed archetypally, that break from the Church reflects the shift from the religious orientation of the Pisces/Virgo era, geared as it was toward self-sacrifice and otherworldly ideals, to that of the Aquarian/Leo era, with its emphasis on secular values and worldly concerns like "life, liberty, and the pursuit of happiness."

That symbolism is essentially the same as that found in the earlier film, *The Jazz Singer*. A technical landmark, that was the first feature-length film to feature fully synchronized sound, and was a tipping point in the way movies were made from that point on. (Its release on October 6, 1927 coincided with the departure of Uranus out of Pisces into 0 degrees Aries – a clear portent of new beginnings.) In a way similar to *The Sound of Music*, the earlier film depicts a character agonizing over a decision to leave a life of religious service behind in order to pursue a secular calling, as a performer in that most Aquarian of musical forms, jazz.

In fact, Maria's story of leaving the Church behind is just one of two interlocking themes in *The Sound of Music* which illustrate the tug of war between Piscean and Aquarian paradigms. In the movie, the von Trapp family finds itself increasingly pressured by the encroaching Nazi regime, and desperately struggles to break free from its oppressive influence. Though the Nazi party displayed some elements of the emerging Aquarian mythos, with its embrace of high technology and mass media, at its heart it embodied the more dogmatic, persecutional aspects of the Piscean Age. Remember, not only was the state religion of Nazi culture Christianity, but its chief icon was a twisted cross – a climactic perversion of Piscean ideals and dogmatism. By contrast, the von Trapps represented the urge toward creative freedom – an impulse clearly aligned with the incoming Aquarius/Leo axis. The Nazi's efforts to squelch their freedom symbolized a desperate last gasp by members of the receding paradigm to subvert the potentials of the burgeoning new one. The movie's happy ending showing the family's escape from Nazi-controlled territory speaks to an ideal of final release from the suffocating grip of a bankrupt older worldview.

2001: A Space Odyssey

As Joseph Campbell pointed out in his classic book, *Hero with a Thousand Faces*, the timeless story of a hero struggling against great odds to obtain a boon or life-changing transformation is found in virtually every culture through history. While the essential message of these tales is much the same, the surface details can change from culture to culture – and it's within those subtle variations that we stand to gain important insights into the worldviews of these cultures.

In earlier times, the obstacle to be overcome may have been a great dragon or supernatural demon, but in Stanley Kubrick's 1968 self-styled "Space Opera," *2001: A Space Odyssey,* our hero must overcome a powerful computer named Hal. (Notice how this name changes when you move each of those letters up a notch in the alphabet—IBM!) "Man versus machine" is a theme that's been echoed by countless science fiction tales through the years, but it's also one of the great problems facing us in the Aquarian Age, as we learn to grapple with the challenges not only of technology but of mechanistic logic – the tendency to perceive the world through a mind-set of pure rationality, devoid of feeling or compassion.

Kubrick's story features an Aquarian message on other levels as well – including a look at our expanded human potential. As I've already mentioned, the coming age will see an emphasis upon the entire Aquarius/Leo axis, because each zodiacal sign is inextricably entwined with its opposite. On one level, this portends a time when ordinary humans could well be transformed into "mini-gods" of a sort, as average men and women awaken to their own heroic potential, in creative, political, and spiritual ways. With a subtle nod to Nietzsche's "Superman" concept – underscored by Kubrick's use of Richard Strauss' music for *Also Sprach Zarathustra* — we see astronaut Bowman traveling through a sort of hyperdimensional stargate, to be eventually reborn, at movie's end, as a mysterious "starchild," shown floating in space above the Earth. In the age ahead, we too could be "lifted up" to levels of higher potential that will fundamentally change our conception of what it means to be human. Will this be brought about through genetic technology, expanded educational techniques, or (as Kubrick's movie suggests) contact with nonhuman intelligence? Stay tuned!

Close Encounters of the Third Kind

The notion of humans being lifted up is a motif that also figures prominently in the myth most associated in the West with the constellation of Aquarius – the Greek tale of Ganymede, the water-bearer. Ganymede was said to have been the most beautiful youth alive. He was watching over his father's sheep one day when he was abducted into the heavens by Zeus, where he became immortalized as a servant to the gods.

It is intriguing that, just as we are about to enter an age governed by a tale of heavenly abduction, we are flooded with accounts from around the world of people being abducted into the sky by celestial beings. True, there have been stories of abductions throughout history – for example, the fairy legends of Celtic lore or the Judaic tale of Enoch's ascension. Yet, this phenomenon has undoubtedly accelerated in recent decades, starting with the famed Betty and Barney Hill case of 1961. Although the abduction motif figures prominently in many of our science fiction films, it found an especially conspicuous expression in Steven Spielberg's 1977 blockbuster movie, *Close Encounters of the Third Kind*, which pivoted around a young boy who was abducted into the sky by nonhuman beings.

The question is: Are these abduction tales based on fact? Or are they simply an expression of our collective fantasies, a result of our overactive imaginations? Fortunately, for our purposes, it doesn't really matter: Either way, we can explore the symbolism of these stories for the insights they offer about the shifting Aquarian zeitgeist. But to do this, we need to explore what "abduction" truly means. Archetypally, abduction refers to a process of becoming caught up in a powerful state of consciousness beyond the control of one's conscious ego, as the psyche is overtaken by mysterious impulses and energies. But there is an important difference between abduction *upward* and abduction *downward*; for instance, the image of Persephone being abducted into the underworld by Pluto suggests getting sucked down into a more emotional, subterranean level of psychic energy. In a sense, whenever we feel overwhelmed by anger, depression, or fear, we've been "abducted into the underworld."

However, the myth of Ganymede features a person being abducted upward into the heavenly realms – a very different implication indeed! This suggests a shift in consciousness that is predominantly mental in character. (Some would see the upward direction as having a more spiritual connotation, but spirituality is more properly related to the balance point represented by the horizon, the proverbial "crack between worlds.") The myth of Ganymede, along with films like Spielberg's *Close Encounters*, may be an omen that humanity could be swept up in an increasingly cerebral mode of experience during the coming Aquarian millennia. This seems especially likely when we stop to consider the element of air associated with Aquarius and its intellectual connotations. At its very best, this shift to the air element could portend a genuine awakening of humanity's higher mind, but it might also point to a more prosaic possibility, as our lives become increasingly dominated by the influence of our media technologies and computers.

Citizen Kane

I mentioned earlier in this book about the extraordinary set of planetary energies accompanying the release of Welles' cinematic *tour de force*. Besides simply reflecting the energies of that period, though, both the style and content of this film offer a mother lode of clues for any astrologer hoping to find insights into the Age-shift currently affecting our world.

In a way similar to *The Truman Show*, *Citizen Kane* speaks to the enormous power of the (Aquarian) media to shape our lives and minds. In the movie, Charles Foster Kane is shown acquiring a newspaper called *The Enquirer*, and shamelessly uses his power to affect lives and manipulate public opinion (shades of Rupert Murdoch!). "People will think what I tell them to think!" he barks at one point, and also, "If the headlines are big enough, the news is big enough!" While mass media has expanded our horizons in important ways, by providing a window to the larger world, films like these illustrate some the serious consequences that can come from misusing our telecommunications technologies, too.

On that note, *Citizen Kane* (again, like *The Truman Show*) also underscores the issue of personal privacy. Throughout the movie, we're shown scenes in which the most intimate details of individual's lives are paraded before a ravenous public. In a scene foreshadowing later scandals like the Bill Clinton/Monica Lewinsky affair, Kane's private tryst with a younger woman is broadcast to the entire world via front-page headlines. Indeed, the entire movie is structured around an investigative reporter's quest to uncover secrets about Kane's personal life, as he seeks to unravel the meaning of Kane's dying word: "Rosebud." As we've increasingly seen in recent years, one of the downsides to our Aquarian high-tech world is that we may all be subject to the prying eyes of information-gathering systems of one sort or another. The three letters that precede our internet sites, "www," may stand for "world wide web," but they could just as well recall those words chanted by protestors back in the 1960s: the whole world is watching!

There is even something Aquarian about the film's narrative style, with its uniquely decentralized, jigsaw-puzzle approach to Kane's character and life. Rather than portray Kane's life from a single perspective, the movie treats us to a wide range of viewpoints about him – including those of his ex-wife, friends, butler, and business associates. As I explore more fully in chapter 12, one of the key metaphoric qualities associated with Aquarius is *decentralization*. Unlike Leo, which symbolically draws things to a central point (like the ruler of a country, or the heart within the human body), Aquarius distributes energy to many centers and hubs, *à la* democracy, the Internet, or the body's arterial system. Similarly, Orson Welles' masterpiece decentralizes the classical narrative into multiple perspectives; by so doing, it foreshadows the cinematic styles of later directors like Robert Altman (*Nashville*) and P. J. Anderson (*Magnolia*).[2] This decentralized quality is also reflected in this movie's pleasure palace, Xanadu, built in a very postmodern style that juxtaposes motifs from many cultures and eras; in that respect, Xanadu could be a metaphor for modern (or postmodern) culture itself.[3]

Fantasia

Walt Disney's 1940 film features a series of animated sequences that illustrate famous pieces of classical music, of which the most iconic (and one that has become virtually emblematic of the Disney empire itself) is "The Sorcerer's Apprentice," set to Paul Dukas' music of the same title. This imaginative episode features several Aquarian resonances worth pondering.

To my mind, the most interesting of these involves the startling stylistic synchronicity between this musical piece and another work composed several years later by Gustav Holst: his "Uranus" suite from the musical composition, *The Planets*. I once heard a musicologist claim there was no clear evidence that Holst ever heard the Dukas piece; but even if he had, it wouldn't explain why Holst chose this particular style to represent the planetary qualities of Uranus. I believe that this synchronicity holds an important symbolic clue to the deeper nature of Uranus itself and its associated Age of Aquarius.

In *Fantasia's* "Sorcerer's Apprentice," we see a character (Mickey Mouse) usurping his teacher's magical powers and tapping into energies far beyond his understanding. In the process, he nearly brings destruction down upon himself (and possibly the entire world). In some sense, this is a fitting description of the role that Uranus has played in modern history, in terms of the energies and technological capacities it's given us access to. In Disney's version of the story about the young apprentice, this awakening of powers is accomplished by means of a magical cap with stars and planets emblazoned on it – yet another Aquarian touch, hinting at the cosmic/celestial knowledge associated with this archetypal principle.

And as with some of our other cinematic examples, we again encounter the familiar "man versus technology" motif: The broom that Mickey Mouse commands to perform his chores runs amok and eventually splits into multiple copies of itself, in a way that almost seems to foreshadow cloning. Notice, too, that while Mickey is being carried away by his fantasies of controlling the world, it is specifically an environmental disaster he sets into motion. Sound familiar?

But perhaps the most important key to the symbolism of this tale lies in the task being performed by those animated brooms – none other than that of "water-bearer"! In the West, the sign of Aquarius is of course the sign of the water-bearer, symbolizing the pouring of hidden energies into manifestation. That Disney's tale specifically hinges on this core image is a remarkable testament to its importance as a cipher into our emerging future. The fact that Disney himself was born with the Sun conjuncting Uranus speaks to his own attunement to the values of that unfolding paradigm.

In the end, Disney offers a depiction of "The Sorcerer's Apprentice" that stands as a cautionary tale for the Aquarian Age, hinting at both the perils and promises of our newly awakened capabilities. While this more obviously applies to such areas as atomic energy and genetics, it may even be relevant to the burgeoning field of "personal empowerment" and the awakening of our psychological potential. Will we use these energies wisely? Or wind up destroying ourselves? One thing Disney's tale makes clear: This isn't a child's game.

Star Wars

George Lucas' now classic film was an overnight sensation when it was first released in 1977. The movie treated audiences to sights and sounds unlike anything they had ever seen before. As a friend of mine remarked at the time, it was almost like stepping into an entirely different world – with its own inhabitants, atmosphere, and even its own logic. Part of the reason for this enormous appeal was, of course, the skillful way that Lucas managed to incorporate the timeless themes of myth and religion into his story and reframe them in the context of space-age technology and values. As such, he crafted a truly Aquarian vision that provided us with a glimpse of humanity's possible future destiny in the stars and the prospect of an interplanetary society.

Further clues into the significance of this film may lie within Lucas' own horoscope and his attunement to futuristic trends. Astrologically, there are several ways to discern a person's degree of alignment with Aquarian themes and symbols; one is the position and quality of Uranus in the horoscope, by sign and aspect. In George Lucas' case, this planet was at 8° Gemini when he was born, on May 14, 1944. This was the same zodiacal point that Uranus inhabited when the Declaration of Independence was signed, on July 4, 1776 (and not far from 24 degrees Gemini, where Uranus was positioned when the planet was discovered several years later, in 1781). In short, George Lucas was born during the United States of America's second Uranus return – a planetary cycle that occurs about every 84 years.

In many respects, America may be seen as the cutting edge of the Aquarian Age itself; its values of freedom, technology, and innovation foreshadow, in microcosm, those of the emerging consciousness. With Lucas' own Uranus plugged directly into the "home" position it occupied in the U.S. chart (and close to this planet's discovery point), Lucas thus has his finger firmly on the pulse of not only American tastes, but those of the era to come.

And from the start, Lucas' work reveals a recurring interest in futuristic themes and technology. His first theatrically released film was titled *THX 1138* and offered a bleak look at the challenges of technology and individualism in the coming age. Several years later, *Star Wars* finally established his reputation as an artistically minded futurist – and a technologically minded businessman. Looking back, it's curious how this movie mirrors the themes and struggles of the Revolutionary War itself, with its group of ragtag, "frontier-style" rebels pitted against a more organized and powerful empire, spearheaded by a great tyrant (in the one case, King George; in the other, Darth Vader). In both cases, the overriding concern is *freedom*. This similarity could hold an omen for our future; if so, America's destiny might well foreshadow that of the Aquarian Age itself. Both the Revolutionary War and Lucas' film will prove to be precursors of coming trends, with their mutual emphasis on attaining independence from depersonalized or oppressive systems – whether governmental, corporate, or technological.

Free Willy

Yes, I'm serious! The archetypes of change express themselves just as much through "low art" as they do through high art, and this 1993 crowd-pleaser is no exception. You don't need to have seen this film to remember the key image associated with it: a killer whale sailing through the air over the head of a young boy. The symbol of a whale gaining freedom was a conspicuous expression of the Uranus–Neptune conjunction that same year, illustrating the blending of planets that rule liberation and oceanic concerns. But remember that these planets also rule the two Great Ages we are presently straddling: Uranus rules Aquarius, and Neptune governs Pisces. In that light, the image of a sea creature escaping confinement and becoming airborne, precisely as these planets were merging, presents us with another symbol of the transformation of consciousness from the old era into the new. Incidentally, this symbol was echoed seven years later by the image of airborne whales in Disney's *Fantasia 2000* (released on the first day of that landmark year).

Of course, the transition between eras is not always quite as smooth as this; the interests of the emerging age sometimes attack those of the older one, rather than tolerating or transforming them. As mentioned in the previous chapter, the U. S. government's destruction of the David Koresh compound in Waco, Texas in 1993 illustrates what can happen when the secular interests of Aquarian society run roughshod over the religious values of a Piscean era. Similarly we also saw the example of Herman Melville's oceanic novel, *Moby Dick*. In Melville's story, a man associated with the whaling industry (sometimes called America's first true industry) sets out to kill a great whale, rather than free it. Here, too, we glimpse the passing of the old Piscean order, but in a way that doesn't allow for a creative appropriation of its lessons and blessings.

Whale Rider

Finally, I'd like to turn to yet another whale-themed film which illustrates a subtly different point – namely, the possibility of bridging the gap between old and new in a harmonious way: the 2002 film from New Zealand, *Whale Rider*. The movie's central character, a young girl from New Zealand's Maori tribe, is struggling to reconcile her burgeoning independence with the conservative traditions of her community. An iconic sequence in the film which embodies that marriage between old and new involves her learning to ride atop a great whale in the ocean.

Needless to say, that image embodies a very different symbolism from that expressed in Herman Melville's *Moby Dick*! To my mind, it speaks to the possibility of drawing on the gifts and legacies of a passing era, rather that simply rejecting them wholesale, and reflects her community's attempt to balance tradition with modernity, and not just a single-minded insistence on one or the other. An emotional high point of the film comes when the young woman delivers a heartfelt speech to her community in which she utters these distinctly Aquarian words, illustrating the intersection of old and new:

> But we can learn, and if the knowledge is given to everyone, then we have lots of leaders, and then soon every one will be strong, not just the ones that have been chosen.

References and Notes

1. Helena Petrovna Blavatsky, *Collected Works XIV*, Wheaton, IL: Theosophical Publishing House, 1985, pp. 54-55.

2. Ten years later, Japanese director Akira Kurosawa extended that stylistic innovation one critical step further with his pioneering film, *Rashomon*, by featuring three completely different versions of the same story, with no clear indication as to which one was "right."

3. As a different level, Welles' story of Charles Foster Kane can be read as a metaphor for the United States itself, and its development over time. Consider some of the parallels: A person is born into rustic, wilderness conditions, but as a fortuitous result of rich natural resources, becomes fabulously wealthy; he's plucked from those modest beginnings and taken over by a bank (!); he becomes a hugely successful force in the

media; he compiles a "Declaration of Principles" (echoing America's Declaration of Independence); and finally winds up having changed from an originally idealistic figure to a bloated and fairly hollow shell of his former self. And just as Kane is shown having had very little real childhood, the U.S., too, had little of the normal evolutionary growth that most other countries around the world have experienced, in terms of evolving slowly from an indigenous culture over centuries and millennia. Rather, the U.S. was essentially a European culture grafted onto North American soil (eradicating much Native American culture in the process) – with the end result being both the best and the worst of what this nation stands for.

On the one hand, that lack of real history or normal emotional development has allowed the U.S. to begin with a blank slate on life and see things afresh, less encumbered by outworn social customs and ideals, leading to a spirit of innovation and freedom. On the other hand, that lack of a true national childhood has led to a certain lack of "soul" that – not unlike Charles Foster Kane – has caused too many Americans to try to fill that emotional void through an endless quest for "things" and superficial entertainments. On that level, Welles' movie is not only a significant work of art but a powerful cautionary tale for the nation that created it – a tale made possible by the rare astrological window in time that birthed it.

Reprinted from *The Mountain Astrologer* magazine, April/May 2003.

11

Wheels of Change:
Stelliums, Mundane Astrology, and the
Art of the Big Picture

In 1499 the German astrologer Johann Stoffler predicted the world would be destroyed by a catastrophic flood on February 4, 1524, due to an ominous conjunction of planets in Pisces, the zodiacal sign of water. It wasn't long before other astrologers quickly followed suit by lending their support to Stoffler's claim of an impending deluge, spurring many to build boats or relocate to higher ground. Even the philosopher Niccolo Machiavelli chimed in at one point by writing verses urging others to escape to the high hills to avoid the coming cataclysm.

As it turned out, 1524 came and went without any catastrophe, and certainly produced no such "flood"– or so it seemed. If we stand back and broaden our historical focus just a bit we'll see that quite a lot happened, actually, but it didn't unfold precisely in 1524, nor was it as straightforward as astrologers of the time predicted.

As befits the symbolism of Pisces, the years and decades which followed witnessed a profound change in the world, but one involving the religious sensibility of men and women, as the once all-powerful Catholic church found itself convulsed by dissent amongst its parishioners and priests. That reached a tipping point ten years later, in 1534, when Martin Luther translated the Bible into German, thus making it available to ordinary people and undercutting the privileged status of papal authority. It would be the beginning of the end for the centralized church, a Copernican shift in the religious world, as it were.

So in reality, a "flood" did occur, but it involved a different manner of Piscean symbolism altogether, and unfolded over a much longer span of time. [1]

Examples like this tell us something important about the nature and symbolism of stelliums, and how they operate in our world. Take a close look at their timing throughout history and you'll find that they rarely exert their full influence right away, tending instead to reveal their true power over years or even decades. In that respect I've come to think of them as "industrial strength New Moons." Ever heard the phrase "what the New Moon promises, the Full Moon delivers"? That's true of all conjunctions, actually, since they represent the starting point of larger cycles. When Pluto and Neptune came together in the early 1890s, for instance, the conjunction planted a seed that continued to unfold in the decades which followed in the areas of religion, technology, and the arts.

So when an entire group of planets comes together to form a multiple-conjunction – what astrologers properly term a stellium – it signals a change of an even more momentous sort, particularly if one or more of the outer planets are involved. Such configurations serve as history's engines of change, indicating seismic shifts in the cultural imagination on multiple levels simultaneously. Whenever they occur throughout the centuries, we see one chapter in the collective consciousness closing off and another one opening up, a proverbial "changing of the guard" in one area or another.

This understanding of planetary line-ups is something that artists, poets and filmmakers through the years have intuitively sensed, as for example in Jim Henson's *Dark Crystal*, or Stanley Kubrick's *2001: A Space Odyssey*, where major shifts in evolution were shown accompanied by major line-ups of planets.

With that in mind, it's worth taking a look at some other significant events from history to see how an understanding of stelliums can shed light on their meaning and timing.

The Events of 9/11

It may have been writer and esoteric scholar Manly Palmer Hall who first suggested that major wars are often accompanied or preceded by major multiple planet line-ups. That isn't simply because stelliums are inherently negative or violent, but because they signal seismic changes in consciousness – of which wars and revolution are the most turbulent expressions. Think of the word "revolution" itself, which is an astronomical term describing the completion of a cycle, of something coming "full circle" then starting up again. The effects of stelliums are revolutionary in the truest sense of the word.

There are countless examples of this from recent history. The Spanish American War was preceded by a six-planet line up in Sagittarius during early December of 1899; the outbreak of World War I was accompanied by a close conjunction of six planets in Aquarius during January of 1914, all within six degrees; America's entry into World War II followed on the heels of a major lineup in Taurus in May of 1941, while the multiple planet lineup of 1962 preceded the nearly-apocalyptic Cuban Missile Crisis later that fall. To that short list I'd add the seven planet line-up that occurred in January of 1994 in Capricorn, followed just a few weeks later by the horrific slaughter in Rwanda of hundreds of thousands of men, women, and children.

So when I learned that a significant line-up of planets was slated to occur in May of 2000, involving the planets Mars, Mercury, Sun, Moon, Venus, Saturn, and Jupiter, all in the earthy sign of Taurus, I wondered whether we'd see a major conflict taking shape in its wake, too. The last time we saw a stellium in Taurus this significant was back in early 1941, the same year we saw the world plunged into a global conflict following the bombing of Pearl Harbor several months later in December.

But if a major conflict was going to unfold this time around, what form would it take? And who would be battling whom, I wondered. I've come to believe we can get an early sense of what a major stellium might bring by looking closely for subtle clues or omens around the time of the alignment itself. That's because even though the full effects of the alignment won't be felt right away, their effects will announce their presence in the form of "seed symbols" early on. Those can show up in any number of places, such as movies, books, TV shows, or other social developments. For example, the twelve months following the Uranus/Neptune conjunction of 1993 saw the emergence into popular consciousness of the internet, a development that has since gone on to alter our world in ways far greater than anyone at the time could have imagined. 1993 was also the year the Hubble Telescope became fully active – a technological marvel that's since gone on to change our understanding of the universe. Anyone paying attention back in the early 1990s could have predicted developments like these could have long-lasting repercussions, simply by merit of the timing involved.

So when I learned that a major Hollywood film was about to be released exactly in the midst of the 2000 stellium, I was curious to see if anything in the film might might hold clues for our near future. Sitting in the movie theater that first weekend, I was particularly struck by the film's opening sequence, which depicted a battle between the Roman legions and barbarians at the Empire's borders. I thought much about that scene in the coming months, and on finishing up my second book *Signs of the Times* one year later, wrote the following passage about what that sequence could portend for the long-range impact of the Taurus stellium:

> ...as of this writing (Spring, 2001), there are disturbing signs of unrest taking shape around the world, particularly in the Middle East, along with growing concerns over terrorist activity directed against the United States by militant factions from that region. Perhaps this uneasiness shows another level of significance in *Gladiator*, released during the May 2000 lineup. In that film's first major sequence, imperial troops battle 'barbarian' forces at the Empire's borders, using their superior technology. Set during the reign of emperor Marcus Aurelius, it is a turning point in the Empire's history; Roman power has reached its zenith, yet it will increasingly find itself threatened by those very barbarians – that era's equivalent to our modern- day 'third world' countries. One might see a parallel here with the state of affairs now facing superpowers like America in its dealings with Iraq or terrorists like Osama bin Laden, though whether we'll see a similar turning of the tide like that experienced by ancient Rome remains to be seen.[2]

As it turned out, the publication date on my book was pushed back from Autumn of 2001 to early 2002 (a not uncommon practice in the publishing field, alas); but fortunately the editors kept that passage intact, however moot it had become by that point. But the fact remains that the tragedy on 9/11 did revolve around terrorists and Osama bin Laden, at least as far the dominant media narrative around the tragedy was concerned. Whatever one's own beliefs about what really happened that day, the attack on the Twin Towers and the Pentagon became the opening volley in the much-ballyhooed "war on terror," which not only impacted life in regions like Iraq, Afghanistan and Pakistan but seriously undermined civil rights in the U.S. as a result of the Patriot Act. As yet another expression of the Taurean symbolism in that stellium, the decade following 9/11 also witnessed a restructuring of the U.S. (and to some extent world) economy, as Bush's term in office made the corporate sector's influence on American politics more far-reaching than ever before.

Since then, of course, many astrologers have gone on to relate 9/11 to the powerhouse opposition between Pluto and Saturn that was in effect throughout 2001 and 2002, due to that aspect's association with high drama and structural transformations. While that configuration surely played a key role in the events of that day, I'd suggest that we view it as superimposed on the lingering effects of the stellium one year earlier, and that the two energies were acting in concert with one another. Historic events are rarely the result of any one planetary pattern by itself, in other words, and it's important that we consider the multiple causes which can pool their energies into a single development, whether that be the Protestant Reformation, 9/11, or Pearl Harbor.[3]

The JFK Assassination and the Beatles

As a child in grade school at the time, I'm old enough to remember exactly where I was when I got the news of JFK's assassination that day. That was a remarkable enough moment in history, but it was made all the more remarkable by the convergence of several other significant events happening in its compass. Consider that less than sixty minutes before the President was shot, the famous Christian theologian and fiction writer C.S. Lewis died, while just twelve minutes before that the famed author and intellectual Aldous Huxley died (famously under the influence of LSD, incidentally).

But that's not all. While doing some research on the music of that period, I came across this extraordinary tidbit on Wikipedia:

> On 10 December 1963, a five-minute news story shot in England about the phenomenon of Beatlemania was shown on the CBS Evening News. The segment first aired on the CBS Morning News on 22 November and had originally been scheduled to be repeated on that day's Evening News, but regular programming was cancelled following the assassination of President John F. Kennedy earlier that day.

In other words, the very same day that JFK was shot and both C.S. Lewis and Aldous Huxley died, North American audiences experienced one of their first media glimpses of a musical phenomenon which eventually went on to define the entire decade – the Beatles.

Clearly, something big was "in the air" that day. But what, exactly?

Astrologers have debated the horoscope of the JFK assassination ever since, and more than a few have puzzled over the seeming lack of major configurations that day. True, Pluto was widely squaring Mercury, Mars, and Venus, while Uranus was closely squaring Mercury as well, along with a few other aspects. But none of these are especially unusual, and certainly not earthshaking. And the Earth definitely shook on 11/22/63. So what could have triggered a tectonic shift the likes of which heralded the demise of Camelot, the death of notable writers, and the introduction of a major musical phenomenon to American audiences?

Rather than look solely at the transits on that day, I'd suggest we broaden our focus and examine the larger trends throughout that entire decade. Notably, the 1960s played host to the once-in-every-110-year conjunction of Uranus and Pluto which became exact in 1965 and 1966 (though its influence extended for years on either side). But no less important was the fact that the decade also witnessed an extraordinary line-up of planets in Aquarius just one year before JFK's assassination, during the first week February, 1962 – a configuration made even more powerful by the inclusion of an exact conjunction of the Sun and Moon, in a solar eclipse.

If we look carefully to where the planets were when JFK was assassinated in 1963 (12:30 PM standard time, November 22, 1963, Dallas, TX), we find that the transits at that moment not only formed significant aspects to the stellium one year earlier but also served to trigger the potentials of the emerging Uranus/Pluto conjunction. Among these triggers were:

- When JFK was shot the planets of the 1962 stellium were crossing over the Ascendant in Dallas, with the Nodes particularly aligned to the November 22 Asc/Dsc axis.

- Transiting Uranus on November 22 was conjuncting Pluto in the 1962 chart.

- The Moon returned to the sign that it occupied back on February 5 of 1962, thus signaling a "lunar return."

- Saturn was squaring the 1962 Venus (and more widely Mercury Jupiter, Sun, and the Moon).

- Transiting Neptune was closely squaring the 1962 Sun.

- Transiting Sun was closely squaring the 1962 Uranus.

In short, the planetary transits on November 22, 1963 were connected to a far broader complex of energies in effect during that entire period, among them the powerful configurations embodied in that stellium back in February of 1962. Like a time-release capsule on a gigantic scale, the extraordinary potentials from that previous year's line-up had been lying in wait, and became activated by the transits on that fateful day in ways that proved both terrifying and inspiring.[4]

Grasping the Big Picture

Examples like these illustrate some of the ways that stelliums demand the need to take the "long view" in assessing their effects long after they've become exact. But this points up an even broader problem that can arise in the astrologer's, practice – namely, the failure to fully consider the big picture when studying virtually any astrological pattern, whether that be on the mundane or personal levels. Let me explain.

As mentioned, when an historic event occurs there's a tendency to zero in on the precise moment it occurred by drawing up a horoscope for that exact minute and hour. Yet that approach runs the risk of missing the proverbial forest for the trees, since there may be far larger patterns at work besides just those isolated transits. Although that's especially true when it come to stelliums, as we've seen, it can happen with other configurations as well.

Take the Uranus/Pluto conjunction of the 1960s. Though it became exact in 1965 and 1966, it continues to exert its effects up through the present day, as evidenced not only in the increasingly liberated attitudes towards sexuality and gender we see amongst younger generations, but in terms of many other dramatic developments that have occurred since then, especially as that conjunction continues being activated by subsequent transits.

In the Spring of 2006, for instance, long after the Uranus and Pluto separated, we suddenly saw many of those born during that conjunction acting out a rebellious energy that strongly recalled the spirit of the 60s, such as with the release of the film *V for Vendetta*, produced by the Wachowski siblings, both born during the Uranus/Pluto conjunction in the mid-60s.[5] The film had its premiere on March 17, 2006, just as transiting Uranus began opposing the zodiacal degrees of the 60's Uranus/Pluto alignment. The fact that we continue seeing street protestors around the world sporting the film's Guy Fawkes mask is a testament not only to the enduring impact of the movie (as well as the Alan Moore graphic novel it's based upon), but to the impact of the Uranus/Pluto conjunction of the mid-1960s. Few astrologers studying the horoscopes for the exact weeks or months of that conjunction back then could have imagined the diverse long-term effects that would continue to result from it over the ensuing decades.

Or consider the square between Uranus and Pluto that we've been dealing with these last few years. It's natural for us to look to the daily news reports for evidence of its effects in real time – and indeed, we've already seen a number of developments that reflect its revolutionary energies in areas like gay marriage, the Occupy Wall Street movement, Arab Spring, drug legalization, and various breakthroughs in the field of science, among others. But the effects of this square will undoubtedly continue to reverberate for months or even years after its completed, as it continues to be triggered by ongoing transits.

To put it simply, when any aspect completes, it isn't "over" – any more than shouting into a canyon stops echoing the moment you close your mouth! Indeed, there's no better example of that than the natal chart itself. As I've often pointed out, one doesn't truly know the full meaning of a planetary configuration until the children born during it grow up and make their mark on the world. For instance, Beethoven was born in the midst of a rare Grand Trine involving the outer planets Uranus, Neptune and Pluto, that came into play during the late 1700s. The effects of that pattern didn't simply evaporate once those planets shifted out of orb! In fact, every time you turn on the radio now and hear the music of Beethoven being played, you're experiencing the effects of the configurations from back then manifesting in the present day.

In that same way, our world is constantly seeing the effects of old planetary configurations in action, both directly and indirectly, through the legacies of figures like Martin Luther King, Julius Ceasar, Plato, Adolph Hitler, or the Buddha. We're all living embodiments of the universe as it appeared at the moment we were born, and we continue to send out those energies through all our actions and achievements. All of which raises an intriguing question: how will the effects of the planetary configurations when *you* were born continue rippling out into the world in the years, decades, or even centuries to come?

Notes

1. In an echo of the 1524 stellium, a more recent planetary line-up in Pisces took place in early 2013, and curiously enough, the Catholic church experienced a significant shift of a different sort then, when Pope Benedict resigned office to be replaced by the incoming Pope Francis. Besides being the first Pope from the Americas, the first Jesuit Pope, as well as the first non-European Pope since Pope Gregory in 741, he's shown himself to be a reformer interested in restoring primary Christian (read: Piscean) principles of compassion and humility, while also showing indications of addressing longstanding financial and sexual abuses in the church. It remains to be seen whether his efforts in that regard will have any lasting effects or not.

2. *Signs of the Times: Unlocking the Symbolic Language of World Events* (Hampton Roads 2002), p. 258.

3. It's worth noting that the 2000 Taurus stellium included a square to the planet Uranus, just as the 1941 Taurus stellium did – and both of the tragedies unfolding in their wakes, Pearl Harbor and 9/11, involved deadly attacks by aircraft.

4. As yet another example of the long-term effects of the 1962 stellium, singer Bob Dylan (himself born at the tail end of a stellium, on May 25, 1941) saw his first album being released the same month as that line-up in Aquarius. It attracted little attention at the time, yet eventually turned out to be the start of an extraordinarily successful career lasting to the present day.

5. Andy Wachowski was born on December 27, 1967, while Lana (formerly Larry) Wachowski was born on June 21, 1965.

Reprinted from *The Mountain Astrologer*, October/November 2014.

12

Drawing Down the Fire of the Gods:
Reflections on the Leo/Aquarius Axis

A picture is worth a thousand words, they say. So when I was asked to distill some ideas for an article on the Leo/Aquarius axis, I immediately thought back to one image that, to my mind, best captured the essence of this zodiacal dynamic:

> Two or three children on a playground, laughing and singing in blissful aban-
> don, while circled around them are a dozen scientists in white lab coats, carefully
> observing and recording every move for a research study on the nature of play.

As with all symbolic images, this one offers a number of diferent levels of meaning, and for that reason provides a useful point of departure for exploring some of the many themes associated with the Leo/Aquarius polarity. As I hope to make clear, understanding this vital zodiacal polarity is not only important for understanding our personal horoscopes, but for unlocking the significance of the pivotal historical period we find ourselves about to enter: the much-heralded Age of Aquarius.

The Dance of Fire and Air

Where does one begin when trying to understand this polarity? One way is to consider the elemental symbolism associated with these signs: Leo represents the principle of fire, while Aquarius represents the principle of air.

First, let's look at fire. Of all the elements, this is the one most associated with life's vitality itself. Like our children romping on the playground, Leonine fire is the principle of pure experientiality, of being-in-the-moment. At its most spiritual, Leo therefore exemplifies the ideals of courage, enthusiasm, and even spontaneous, enlightened awareness. The Buddhists have a saying: "Spontane-ity is the mark of the Buddha." Leo embodies this spontaneous, playful aware-ness at its most dynamic, with its fixity compressing this essence and burnish-ing it to a diamond-like brilliance. At its worst, this same principle can express itself as self-centeredness or an inability to stand outside one's own perspective in order to see things – or oneself – objectively.

On the other end of things, Aquarius expresses the principle of air, the ele-ment most associated with the principle of rationality, and mind. Like those scientists on the fringes of our hypothetical playground, air stands outside the field of activity to best observe and conceptualize it and systematically relate it to other ideas and systems. In contrast with the fiery principle of pure being, Aquarian air represents the principle of *understanding*.

At its highest, Aquarian air therefore confers the objectivity and the discernment necessary for effective decision-making, planning, and clear communication. Your ability to read these words right now are made possible through the mediating element of air. But at its worst, Aquarian air can be detached to the point of coldness, standing so far outside of direct experience that it loses touch with the emotional realities of both oneself and others. The famed detachment of Aquarian former president Ronald Reagan offers an example of this.

But how exactly do these different archetypes interact with one another? Traditional astrology informs us that fire and air are complementary and feed one another in symbiotic ways. But, as we shall soon see, the truth of the matter can be far more complex than this.

The Individual/Group Dynamic

As individuals, how do we reconcile our own needs or behaviors with those of the group? And in turn, how does the group impact on our personal lives?

These are just a few of the concerns driving this zodiacal polarity. On the one hand, Leo stands for the principle of the reigning individual, shining before all in his or her uniqueness. At the other end, Aquarius is the common person, mingling with the masses. In political astrology, Leo is therefore associated with government by monarchy or theocracy, where power is focused in a single royal or religious figure, while Aquarius relates to democracy and government by the common man/woman. In short, Leo rules from the top down, whereas Aquarius rules from the bottom up.

Whenever this zodiacal polarity is prominently displayed in someone's horoscope, we often see a concern with integrating personal values with those of the collective. When Leo is more dominant (say, by planetary emphasis), individuals might gravitate toward positions of eminence, toward being the ringleader in social undertakings; but with Aquarius more emphasized, the individual may feel a greater attunement with the group, the masses.

Sometimes, the house placements involved hold the decisive clues as to which direction this will take. For instance, one client of mine had multiple planets in Leo positioned in the 1st house, opposing Aquarius planets in the 7th. Throughout her life she found fulfillment as a charismatic motivational speaker standing before hundreds or even thousands of people. With Leo so prominent in the 1st house, she enjoyed the role of "star" to the hilt. Yet another client of mine had virtually the same planets in the same signs, except positioned in precisely opposite houses (Leo on the 7th, Aquarius on the 1st). For her, this polarity manifested as the compulsion to attend workshops led by charismatic figures and to identify with the masses rather than take on the starring role herself.

On the global scale, planetary configurations involving these two signs often bring about historical events which dramatize that group/individual dynamic *en masse*. When Leo is dominant over Aquarius, for example, there may be events which highlight the ability of lone rulers or nations to affect larger collectives, constructively or destructively. As one example, a much-talked about solar eclipse in August of 1999 featured a powerful Sun-Moon conjunction in Leo, and opposing planets in Aquarius — Leo dominant over Aquarius, in other words. On the exact day of the Full Moon after that eclipse (traditionally, a major trigger mechanisms for eclipses), Chicago's O'Hare airport, one of the world's largest, was essentially shut down for hours because of a lone individual bolting the wrong way through a security checkpoint. As one TV commentator remarked later that evening, "This incident illustrates how a single individual can disrupt the entire system."

On the other hand, a good example of how the collective might impact the life of a single individual or leader would be the Gulf War of 1991. The most significant outer-planet aspect taking place during this conflict was Saturn in Aquarius opposite Jupiter in Leo. (The war itself lasted from mid January to early April; the Jupiter-Saturn opposition was exact on March 15, 1991.) This powerful dynamic found explicit expression in the host of international players involved in the conflict: George Bush and his coalition of nations (Saturn in Aquarius), collectively setting limits on the expansionist ambitions of a renegade would-be king, Saddam Hussein (Jupiter in Leo). In a stunning example of historical synchronicity, this event was paralleled by another development that erupted into public attention during that same period: the Rodney King incident, which came to light in early March. In a manner closely analogous to the United Nations' actions toward Hussein, this urban incident likewise involved a band of disciplinary figures (Los Angeles policemen) beating down on a lone "expansionist" figure, a speeding motorist – by the last name of "King," no less!

With the slow rise of the Aquarian Age, we are already seeing the erosion of longstanding monarchies, and their replacement by democratic forms of government. And in many of these instances, we find powerful configurations occurring in the signs Leo and Aquarius as well. To cite a classic case, all of the major events of the French Revolution occurred in tandem with powerful astrological aspects between Leo and Aquarius (chiefly centering around a major Uranus-Pluto opposition of the period). [1]

A contemporary expression of this same archetypal trend has been the increasingly aggressive behavior of the media toward royalty in recent decades. A prime example was the tragic death of Princess Diana in 1997. On hearing news of her fatal accident while being pursued by paparazzi, I remarked to the person with me at the time that it would be worth looking for any oppositions between Leo and Aquarius at the moment of the crash (Leo ruling royalty and Aquarius ruling the mass media). "In fact," I added, "it would be especially fitting if the Moon turned out to be in Leo, since Princess Di is a symbol of female royalty." Lo and behold, on drawing up the horoscope for August 31, 1997 (12:25 AM CED; Paris, France), that's precisely what I found: Moon in Leo opposing planets in Aquarius.

Stardom/Privacy

Princess Diana's life and death call attention to another expression of the Leo/Aquarius axis in our own time, that of the curious phenomenon of celebrity. As suggested earlier, Leo is the sign most commonly associated with society's "stars" – and quite fittingly, too, since it's the only sign governed by an actual star rather than a planetary body. In older times, the stars of our world generally consisted of political or religious leaders of one stripe or another. But with the advent of modern telecommunications and pop culture, we've witnessed a newfound democratization of celebrity, with the opportunity for ordinary people to rise up out of complete obscurity into positions of fame. Theoretically, at least, anyone can become an object of worship now, and attain their own "fifteen minutes of fame," as (Leo) Andy Warhol described it. Disposable deities, you might say.

But this newfound opportunity provided by mass media, telecommunications, and social media, comes with a price. While each person now has access to the eyes and ears of the world, so the eyes and ears of the world now have growing access to our personal lives, through information about our spending habits via credit cards, our communications through phone records and Internet messages, and even data about our actions in public places via surveillance cameras and spy satellites. Movies like *Enemy of the State* or *The Truman Show* dramatize this predicament through stories of individuals whose personal lives are subjected to pervasive high-tech surveillance.

Creativity

Another key concern of the Leo/Aquarius axis centers around the expression of creativity in our lives. At the one end, Leo expresses the notion of personalized creativity – the lone artist painting in his loft, or the musician composing at her piano, for instance. On the other hand, Aquarius governs all forms of group creativity, where individuals band together to merge their creative energies toward a single project. A modern example of this would be an average film production, where one might find literally hundreds of individuals pooling their energies toward creating one movie.

In actual practice, of course, the notion of "group creativity" is a double-edged sword. At its best, it gives us ensemble work of the most brilliant type, as with films like *The Godfather*, *Citizen Kane*, or *2001: A Space Odyssey*, or through popular musical groups like the Beatles. To my mind, the modern symbol that best captures the essence of Aquarian group creativity is that uniquely American art form, jazz. In contrast to Piscean-Age art forms like the Gregorian choir, where individual creativity is surrendered to a higher ideal, the jazz band encourages group cooperation without denying individual creativity. A thematic structure is still followed, yet it's loose enough to allow for personal freedom of expression. That's a description which also applies, incidentally, to the political structure of a nation like the United States, with its 50 independent states that adhere to a federal constitution. On a technological level, Aquarian Thomas Edison pioneered a jazz-type approach to innovation with the unique workshop environment he developed, which saw an entire team of thinkers pooling their efforts toward conceiving new inventions.

At its worst, the notion of group creativity calls up images of faceless bureaucracies, or "beehive" societies, where individual creativity is essentially squashed by the collective machinery. One doesn't have to look far to find examples from our own time of the way creativity has become constrained by corporations and the "vested interests of the stockholders," to cite just two cases. Nowadays, independent artists find themselves faced with the Faustian bargain of compromising their visions by having to contend with virtual armies of marketing consultants, corporate bureaucrats, and test audiences to get their work out into the marketplace.

But as bleak a scenario as this may seem, I believe there is still reason for hope. While there's no doubt the world has become more corporatized, we still manage to see impressive books, films, and musical compositions emerging out of the system with some regularity. Also, the Internet has introduced a new wrinkle by allowing independent artists to use modern telecommunications for displaying their works before a worldwide audience, thus bypassing the corporate distribution process. Even in the corporate setting, the "jazz" approach has had an impact on the managerial styles of some businesses, with lower- and middle-level employees given greater input in running their companies. So while we have a long way to go, to paraphrase Mark Twain, reports of the death of modern creativity may well be greatly exaggerated.

Pleasure

A close cousin to creativity on our chain of correspondences is the notion of pleasure, with each end of the Leo/Aquarius polarity approaching this area in its own unique way. For instance, Leo governs pleasures of a more personal sort, such as with adults having a romantic affair, or children romping on our proverbial playground. By contrast, Aquarius governs *group* pleasures involving many individuals together, as we might see in a theme park like Disneyland or Universal Studios. In such environments groups of individuals come together and might take a virtual ride into outer space, venture down simulated jungle rapids, or thrill at the sight of electronic dinosaurs clawing at them. But perhaps the most

pervasive form of Aquarian pleasure in our time is that of mass entertainment, expressed through media forms like films, TV shows, or radio
broadcasts. With a television show, for instance, it's possible for millions
or even billions of people around the world to enjoy the same show at
the exact same moment.

Examples like this point up several other key aspects of Aquarian
pleasure, such as its heavily technological nature – as with video games,
virtual reality devices, and Internet chat rooms – not to mention its more
cerebral character. As an extreme example, just imagine an Internet party
of astrophysicists swapping jokes about the Grand Unified Theory! In
contrast with the immediacy of Leonine play, Aquarian pleasure generally involves an element of detachment where the participant is somehow
removed from the heart of experience. Not unlike our scientists standing
outside of the playground looking in, an average TV viewer experiences
the action vicariously and indirectly, more as a spectator than a player.
And notice the impersonality implied here as well: With an ordinary
television show, you can have literally millions of viewers sitting around
at the same moment, watching the same event – yet all of them are completely separate from one another. So it may well be that the Aquarian
Age will usher in a time when we all "come together as one" – though
this could well take a more technological turn than many are expecting.

Chance

In traditional astrology, gambling is said to fall under the rulership of the
5th house in the chart – the house naturally associated with Leo;[2] To my
mind, this has always concealed a deep esoteric truth. Why? Because in
addition to being a form of play, gambling – like most of the other areas
we've been exploring thus far – involves a certain element of chance, of
randomness. For whether we talk about romance, creativity, conception,
or childbirth, we are, in each case, looking at something essentially spontaneous and unpredictable. Conceiving a child is one of life's greatest
crapshoots, not only in terms of whether pregnancy will occur but as far
as the kind of child one might bring into the world.

Correspondences like that open a window onto a deeper truth of both
Leo and the 5th house, namely, that the spontaneity expressed in these
areas reflects the free-flowing qualities of Spirit itself, of that innermost
fount of consciousness where energy unfolds openly and intuitively, un-

fettered by logic or calculation. In moments of play or creativity, we tap into this divine, creative source of being; that's even reflected in our use of the term re-creation when describing ordinary pastimes. Gambling likewise stems from this same divine impulse, though for more distorted and self-aggrandizing reasons.

So how does this principle of spontaneity or chance manifest when filtered through the opposite sign of Aquarius? For one, it gives rise to mass games of chance, as well as technological and corporatized forms of chance. In stark contrast with the more traditional scene of a few individuals standing around throwing dice into the dirt, the emerging Great Age has already introduced bustling amphitheaters that accommodate thousands of individuals playing electronic slot machines side by side. The house of worship for many these days is a modern-day shrine to chance like a Las Vegas casino, where an entirely new different of gods is invoked in the hope of altering one's fate. In a more positive way, our earlier example of the jazz band might reflects a more Aquarian approach to chance, since it's based on the concept of group improvisation, a creative form based on one's response to the unpredictabilities of each moment.

Environments like Disneyland or Las Vegas also express a distinctively Aquarian approach to chance in their shared concern with controlling the unpredictable. At an amusement park like Disneyland, for example, engineers take activities which traditionally involved huge elements of risk and bring them under tight supervision, in order to best provide the customer with all the thrills and vicarious enjoyments of chance-laden experiences, but without all the messy randomness and unpredictability. Rather than risk one's life going out on a big-game safari, one can experience a simulated version of the same thing, all from the safety of your electronically guided car.

And, while childbirth has always been one of life's more unpredictable activities, scientists are learning how to reduce the element of chance there as well, with new advances in fertilization and genetic engineering. The striking film, *Gattaca*, features a scene that beautifully illustrates this dilemma: Set at an unspecified point in our future, a couple comes into a fertility clinic to consult with a corporate counselor on planning out the features of their next child. The counselor tries to convince them to go all the way and pick out every characteristic of their future child; but they are resistant, wondering if it wouldn't be nice to leave just a little bit to chance and randomness. The counselor seems perplexed as to why anyone would even want to leave any part of the conception process to chance. In much the same way, the Aquarian society of our future may be one where, for better or worse, we attempt to control as many elements of randomness and unpredictability in our world as possible – in short, to harness chance.

This same archetypal polarity may also explain efforts by modern scientists to unlock the "laws of chance" in many different shapes and forms. Entire disciplines have sprung up over the last century which attempt to uncover the hidden order beneath life's apparent randomness. These disciplines include statistical theory, Quantum Physics with its notions of "probability theory," the revolutionary new science of Chaos (complexity), and even the emerging field of synchronicity studies. Consider Chaos theory, for example. Researchers contend that by carefully observing the complex behaviors of phenomena previously thought to be purely random (say, the behavior of motorists on a freeway or gas molecules moving about a room), it's possible to discern the hidden laws that govern these patterns.

In our personal horoscopes, significant aspects between the signs Leo and Aquarius sometimes indicate an effort to balance personal spontaneity with the restrictions of social convention. At their most constructive, our collective behavioral codes serve to channel or restrain the wilder expressions of our fiery personal impulses – the result being a little something we call "civilization." In our own horoscopes, configurations between Leo and Aquarius can act themselves out through our interactions with those around us, with others mirroring back one or the other extreme of that polarity. As just one example, individuals with a prominent Leo/Aquarius might themselves be largely spontaneous, while their spouses or business partners might be heavily rational or detached in their temperament, or vice versa.

The One and the Many

Another metaphor that I find useful in explaining the distinction between Leo and Aquarius draws from the field of medical astrology. Traditionally, Leo is associated with the heart while Aquarius is often associated with the distribution of the blood via the arteries. Viewed symbolically, that tells us an important insight into the archetypal processes underlying these two signs. Simply put, Leo is the principle of centralization, while Aquarius is the principle of decentralization.

This dynamic helps explain several of the areas we have been looking at thus far. For instance, when we say that Leo rules government by monarchy, we understand it is because monarchy centralizes the power of the nation into a single king or queen, who is analogously the "heart" of a country; by contrast, democracy decentralizes power to the furthermost "branches" of society, i.e., ordinary men and women. Whereas Leo is the principle of the One, Aquarius is therefore the principle of the Many. Or think of this visual analogy: Leo may be compared with pure white light, while Aquarius could be compared to the prismatic breaking up of light into multiple colors, into a spectrum. Hence, while Leo is more monolithic in focus, Aquarius has a more kaleidoscopic agenda, with its greater emphasis on diversity.

In light of such correspondences, it is not hard to understand why Aquarius is symbolically linked to systems, networks, and associations of all kinds. On the global scale, that may suggest that the next Great Age will be an era of complex alliances and networks of many types – political, social, or technological. Systems within systems within systems. We even see the multi-perspective qualities of Aquarius in such modern developments as postmodernism, with its splintering of traditional Truth into multiple truths and world views.

When unity-minded Leo is added to the Aquarian mix, we find a concern with creative networking, or with unifying diverse elements into an overarching network. Examples of this on the collective scale would be organizations like Jesse Jackson's "Rainbow Coalition" or the United Nations, where we see diverse peoples or races joined together in their common interests. On the level of personal horoscopes, this axis is often emphasized in the charts of thinkers or philosophers with a capacity for synthesizing diverse ideas and intellectual systems within unifying paradigms. Examples of this would be Carl Jung (July 26, 1875), H.P. Blavatsky (August 12, 1831), Alfred North Whitehead (February 15, 1888), and the founder of psychosynthesis, Roberto Assagioli (February 27, 1888), all of whom suggested new ways of synthesizing or reframing traditional ideas. A more recent example would be transpersonal psychologist Ken Wilber (January 31, 1949), whose horoscope features a prominent link between these two signs. Over the last two decades, Wilber has been involved with synthesizing diverse systems into unifying frameworks of various types. Fittingly, perhaps, the title of his first published book was *The Spectrum of Consciousness*.

Leo and Aquarius in the Chakra System

I believe it's possible to uncover a still deeper level of meaning to this zodiacal polarity, by considering where it falls in the context of the yogic chakra system. As I discussed in chapter 6, many esotericists, both East and West, have suggested a close relationship between astrological symbols and the psycho-spiritual system of the chakras. According to this set of correspondences, Leo is associated with the point of the "third eye" (Ajna chakra), while Aquarius relates to one side of the lowest "root" chakra (Muladhara).

Correspondences like these reveal new insights into the host of associations we've been examining thus far. With Leo, for instance, traditional associations like creativity, pleasure, spontaneity, or even centralization all take on added significance as echoes of the spiritual center at the level of the forehead, commonly described as the seat of creative, visionary consciousness. On the other hand, the scientific detachment of Aquarius assumes new meaning when viewed in relation to the root (Saturn) chakra, the point of the chakric ladder farthest away from the third eye. Like our scientists on the outside of the playground looking in, consciousness at this level is likewise "outside looking in" relative to the playground of pure being concentrated in the Ajna chakra. (Remember, "upper" or "lower" in the chakric hierarchy does not mean "better" or "worse" in any absolute sense, since each chakric level has its own spiritual or unspiritual modes of expression.)

Power, Will, and the Promethean Axis

Also consider the closeness of this zodiacal axis to the central spinal column, referred to by yogis as the sushumna, the pathway of kundalini energy. While it would be wrong to suggest the Leo/Aquarius axis is identical to the kundalini force (Leo/Aquarius being more masculine and forceful in quality, and more akin to what the yogis refer to as the "right hand" channel of pingali), it arguably comes closer than any other polarity in the zodiac. As anyone who has studied charts for any length of time knows, the Leo/Aquarius axis (and its corollary planetary aspect,

Sun conjunct Uranus) taps into something profound within our nature, something closely related to consciousness itself at its most dynamic and luminous.[3] Might this even explains why imagery of laser beams or "light sabers" have come to hold such power for movie audiences these days, as we shift into the next Great Age?

As this polarity expresses itself through the Aquarian end, we often find a hidden urge with this sign to take "higher" energies and apply them to everyday situations, as in the case of an inventor. A modern technology sometimes associated with the Leo/Aquarius polarity is that of solar power, and, to my mind, that offers a useful symbol for understanding the archetypal dynamics underlying this polarity. In the same way that solar power technology "draws down" energy from the Sun for use in everyday life, so Aquarius may be said to "draw down" energy from the Ajna chakra into the realm of physical-plane concerns. For this reason, we might call the Leo/Aquarius polarity the *Promethean axis* – Prometheus being the mythological figure who carried fire down from Mt. Olympus to humanity.[4]

As we shift into the Aquarian Age, we see numerous ways in which "fire" is already being "drawn down from the mountain top" into daily affairs: politically, through democracy; economically, through a capitalistic system that shifts wealth from a ruling elite into the hands of ordinary entrepreneurs; technologically, through electricity which makes the once awesome power of lightning available through small holes in the walls of our homes, or through atomic power, which literally harnesses the powers of the Sun for human use; and intellectually, through the democratization of knowledge made possible through books, magazines, and the Internet. In recent centuries, we've even seen renewed interest in the Prometheus myth itself, as with the writings of Percy Shelley (*Prometheus Unbound*), or his wife's famed novel, *Frankenstein* (originally subtitled *The Modern Prometheus*), which continues to captivate audiences with each new generation.

Yet, as Mary Shelley's story of Dr. Frankenstein also shows, great power is accompanied by great responsibilities as well as great dangers. The Leo/Aquarius axis may well be called the "third rail" of the zodiac, since tapping into it can be an electrifying, even lethal experience. Classical mythology offers numerous warnings about the problems of unwisely acquired powers, of course, but during the last century we've witnessed countless real-life examples of what happens when power is wielded without the counterbalancing forces of feminine compassion or reflectivity. The ability of a commoner like Hitler to rise from the lowest ranks of society into a position of global power is only one testament to the perils of "playing with fire," politically or psychologically. Hiroshima and Chernobyl offer equally dramatic examples of this danger on more technological and scientific levels.

In terms of what this axis indicates in personal charts, one could speculate about the alternately tyrannical/subversive streak that sometimes accompanies this polarity. But while that wouldn't be entirely wrong, the problem with it is, it's only one piece of a much larger puzzle. So when consulting with clients, it is always important to note the considerable positive potentials contained in this axis as well – creatively, socially, intellectually, and, as we are about to see, spiritually.

The Mystery of the Sphinx

The metaphor of solar power provides us with one last insight into Leo/Aquarius experience, that involving its unique relationship to mysticism. Just as solar power draws down the fires of the Sun into everyday use, the Leo/Aquarius polarity concerns the drawing down of "spiritual fire" from higher states into more personalized contexts, such as through a more individualized approach to spirituality. In pre-scientific cultures, for instance, "Divinity" was viewed in largely Leonine terms as residing in certain individuals like the King, Pope, or a God utterly beyond ourselves. But with the emerging Aquarian mythos, we are increasingly seeing the democratization of divinity, where Spirit is recognized to reside with each man, each woman.

In personal horoscopes, an emphasis on the Leo/Aquarius polarity often signals an interest in "personal empowerment," either in spiritual or psychological ways. The chart of TV talk show host Oprah Winfrey (January 29, 1954) features a powerful configuration between Aquarius and Leo, for instance.

At its most sublime, the harmonizing of Leo and Aquarius expresses a truth that holds special relevance for men and women of our time: *the reconciliation of the divine and the human.* At the outset of this chapter I proposed one image to convey some of the qualities of this zodiacal dynamic. In closing, I would suggest another, very different symbol to express the perfect integration of these polar opposites: the Egyptian sphinx. In this timeless image we see the merging of the lion and the human bodies into one. However the Egyptians themselves may have intended this symbol (and there isn't complete agreement even among Egyptologists on that point), it's possible that the growing interest we've seen in this archeological wonder during recent decades stems directly from its archetypal numinosity as an emblem for our emerging spiritual potentials.[5] This was something William Butler Yeats seemed to have anticipated even a century ago, when he penned these lines in his poem that anticipated (or bemoaned?) the coming Aquarian Age, "The Second Coming":

> Surely some revelation is at hand;
> Surely the Second Coming is at hand.
> The Second Coming! Hardly are those words out
> When a vast image out of Spiritus Mundi
> Troubles my sight: somewhere in sands of the desert
> A shape with lion body and the head of a man .... [6]

Notes

1. There is some controversy whether it is appropriate to relate configurations taking place in tropical Aquarius with the essentially sidereal Aquarian Age, since these have become dislocated from one another through time, due to the "sliding zodiac" problem. It's my own belief that there is always a symbolic resonance between the tropical and sidereal versions of any sign, even when widely separated from one another – though that connection is undoubtedly stronger when the two signs in question are exactly synchronized (as happened roughly 2,000 years ago).

2. By sign and house rulership, gambling is associated with Leo and the 5th house, while, by planet, it is associated with Jupiter.

3. The entire fixed axis (Leo/Aquarius/Taurus/Scorpio) is closely associated with psycho-spiritual "power," but with certain distinctions between the dual polarities involved. The Leo/Aquarius axis expresses a more masculine, outwardly forceful aspect of consciousness, whereas the Taurus/Scorpio axis expresses a comparatively feminine and more emotional aspect of spiritual power. In the context of the chakras, this

distinction is visible in the way Leo/Aquarius is more aligned with the vertical path of the spine, whereas Taurus/Scorpio extends out horizontally toward the secondary channels of ida and pingali – the domain of shakti, or cosmic feminine energy.

4. My use of the Prometheus story in describing the Leo/Aquarius axis is partly inspired by Richard Tarnas' insightful writings on Prometheus and Uranus, though I've applied them here in a zodiacal context. Tarnas' views can be found in his book, *Prometheus the Awakener: An Essay on the Archetypal Meaning of the Planet Uranus*, Woodstock, CT: Spring Publications, 1995.

5. There have been numerous efforts in recent years to determine whether undiscovered chambers may still lie beneath (or around) the Sphinx, most of them inspired by Edgar Cayce's prediction about a great "Hall of Records" coming to light at the end of the 20th century. Whether or not any such records exist at this point beneath the Sphinx, there is good reason to believe that important findings of some sort await us in this area. Should any of these turn out to be revolutionary in significance, it's safe to say their discovery would represent important milestones in the unfolding Aquarian mythos, and should be examined in terms of their astrological timing.

6. Willam Butler Yeats, "The Second Coming," *The Collected Poems of W.B. Yeats*, New York, NY: Macmillan Publishing Co., Inc., 1974.

Reprinted from *The Mountain Astrologer*, February/March 2000.

13

Tuning into the Zeitgeist:
Riding the Waves of Planetary Change

Late in the summer of 1992, while working for a magazine outside of Chicago, I began feeling increasingly burned out by the long hours I'd been keeping for months on end, and decided to just get away for a few days by myself. So, after talking it over with both my bosses, I managed to wrangle a few extra days around an upcoming weekend and rearrange a few other things in my schedule. It was all very spontaneous, but something about it felt right, as though this was exactly the right thing to do, and the best time to do it.

But where to go? I'd been thinking for some time about a historical site in South Dakota I'd read about years before, called Bear Butte. Of all the sites revered by the Native American Plains Indians, this one seems to hold a special importance – a 1,200-foot hill where 60-plus tribes from the United States and Canada still come to conduct vision quests and spiritual retreats. For some reason, something was calling me to this spot more than any other right now. So, late that following Friday afternoon after work, I headed out on the highway toward the northern Great Plains, the Black Hills fixed firmly in my sights.

Driving on just a little sleep, I managed to make it across the border of South Dakota sometime the next day, and eventually reached my destination. This whole area is rich in history, I came to learn, having played host to such iconic figures as Sitting Bull, Crazy Horse, and Red Cloud. In 1857, a council of Indian nations met at Bear Butte to discuss the problem of white settlers putting down stakes in the region – but to little effect. Sad ghosts linger around these parts. After climbing to the top of the hill and spending some time by myself, interrupted only once or twice by other hikers coming along, I made my way back down and spent the next couple of days exploring the area around Bear Butte, including Mount Rushmore and the nearby city of Sturgis. After two whirlwind days, I got into my car and drove on back to Chicago, feeling noticeably rejuvenated.

It was just a few days later, after settling back in at work, that an odd thing happened. While conversing with a few individuals, both in person and over the phone, I discovered that at least three other people besides myself made the long trek to Bear Butte the same weekend I did, all completely independent of one another! That four different people would all be drawn to the same remote spot on the exact same weekend (and not even cross paths with one another) seemed startling to me, almost as though we were all pulled there by some unseen force. There's even some small irony in the fact that Bear Butte is just a proverbial stone's throw from Devil's Tower, the site where Spielberg filmed *Close Encounters of the Third Kind* – a movie about individuals mysteriously drawn to the same geographical spot by some unknown force. Irony, synchronicity, call it whatever you like.

I've had a number of experiences like this over the years, where I found myself attracted to a place or subject around the same time as others, in ways that were difficult to explain. Not impossible, just difficult. And every one of these times, I've been reminded of the subterranean links that synchronicity always seems to hint at, as though our lives have been choreographed in ways we can scarcely imagine, with subtle connections drawing together seemingly disparate events and people.

And among other things, this prompted me to wonder about the true nature of thoughts. What are they, really? And where do they come from? Are they simply generated by our brains, as most scientists claim? Or do we pick them up out of the ethers, almost like radio waves captured by a receiver? While still a teenager, I came across this intriguing quote attributed to anomalist Charles Fort (though its exact source is debated); it resonated with me then, and still does now:

> … ours is an organic existence, and … our thoughts are the phenomena of its eras, quite as its rocks and trees and forms of life are.

That crystallized my own view precisely, since I'd already wondered even by that young age if my ideas might somehow be a product of my time and place, rather than something strictly personal to me. In that same spirit, I now had to wonder whether it was possible I'd simply tuned into the same "Bear Butte" wavelength those other three people had tuned into that weekend back in 1992. At the very least, it was food for thought.

The Zeitgeist

Philosophers have a word for this sort of thing – *zeitgeist*, or "spirit of the age." Throughout my life, I've noticed how different periods seem to exude distinctly different qualities or moods, and how certain ideas or achievements seem appropriate to their times. A shift in the group consciousness takes place, and suddenly a particular subject becomes all the rage, or certain themes start popping up in different places independent from one another. Historians have long mused over the curious way parallel developments arise simultaneously in independent fields, like inventions appearing at the same time or theoretical breakthroughs being conceived by different people simultaneously, such as Alfred Wallace and Charles Darwin both coming up with evolutionary theory, or Gottfried Leibniz and Isaac Newton both conceiving of calculus.

This happens in the arts, too, perhaps because creative types possess especially sensitive antennae for picking up on subtle trends streaming through the collective consciousness. I once read an interview with songwriter Paul Simon where he marveled at the coincidental way Paul McCartney composed "Let It Be" around the same time that Simon composed "Bridge over Troubled Waters," since the two songs were so similar in tone and completely different from everything else being played on the radio at the time – yet neither he nor Paul was aware of what the other was composing then. Another example would be Bob Dylan releaing his album *Time out of Mind* on the same day as the 9/11 tragedy, with one song on that album ("Mississippi") featuring the uncanny line: "Sky full of fire, pain pouring down." The release date for this CD was planned months in advance by corporate executives, whose decision-making was no doubt strictly practical in nature. So, what really was driving the decision about a release date?

The Astrological Key

Fortunately, astrologers have something of an edge in studying the zeitgeist, since they're able to chart its various waves and shifting currents with some degree of precision. More often than not, that changing mental/emotional atmosphere shows itself to be especially connected with the interactions of the slower-moving planets – in particular, Uranus, Neptune, and Pluto, though Saturn and Jupiter are sometimes involved, too.

For instance, in his book *Cosmos and Psyche*, Richard Tarnas points out that the famed mutiny on the Bounty took place exactly as the French Revolution was erupting in France thousands of miles away. These two events were uniquely parallel to one another in significance, involving nearly unprecedented rebellions against authority, yet there was no way the disgruntled sailors could have known about the French uprising unfolding far away; it's as if both groups were responding to the same revolutionary impulse streaming through the air at the time. But what was that, astrologically? Most likely, the result of a powerful opposition taking place between Uranus and Pluto, two planets traditionally associated with revolutionary energies whenever they join forces.

On that occasion, it was an opposition at work, stirring up turbulent feelings amongst the populace, but for many astrologers an even more profound agent of historical change is the conjunction between slow-moving bodies. During my own life, I've been lucky enough to witness two such pairings of the outer planets: the alignment of Uranus with Pluto during the mid 1960s and the conjunction of Uranus with Neptune during the early 90s. (Lest we take astronomical events like this for granted, keep in mind that there won't be another such conjunction between any two outer planets for rest of this coming century!)

Anyone who's lived through these two periods will know what extraordinary times they were in some ways – politically, scientifically, culturally. The 60s were a period of revolutionary fervor, when people around the world were exploring new ways of thinking about their lives and values. Men walked on the Moon, women and minorities were demanding their rights, and new artistic forms were breaking into consciousness. In popular music, Bob Dylan and the Beatles composed arguably their greatest work precisely as Uranus and Pluto joined forces in 1965 and 1966: Dylan came out with three of his greatest albums (*Bringing It All Back Home*, *Highway 61*, and *Blonde on Blonde*) within the span of those two years, while the Beatles produced *Help!*, *Rubber Soul*, and *Revolver* during that same span of time, with *Sergeant Pepper* following immediately on its heels the next year. This was a period when many other musicians and songwriters were hitting their stride, too, including the Rolling Stones, Joni Mitchell, Buffalo Springfield, the Kinks, and the Beach Boys, to name just a few.

The 1990s, too, were a fascinating time of new influences and revolutionary change, though in somewhat different ways. The Internet exploded into mass awareness during the 12 months following the exact conjunction of Uranus and Neptune in 1993 – and the world hasn't been the same since. The Hubble Space Telescope became operational in 1993, revolutionizing not only our understanding of the universe but our place in it. In the arts, the phenomenon of "world music" was climaxing, with artistic influences from around the globe suddenly becoming hot properties, exemplified by groups like Dead Can Dance. In the publishing field, previously obscure spiritual teachings were now filtering into the mainstream as a result of magazines like *Gnosis* and *The Quest*, along with books like Sogyal Rimpoche's *Tibetan Book of Living and Dying*. A pungent mood of exoticism permeated this entire decade, as exemplified by TV shows like *The X Files* and a growing fascination with mysteries of all types – shamanic, Native American, Egyptian, metaphysical.

The conclusion seems inescapable: The zeitgeist is richer and more creatively potent at some times more than others. During such periods, emotions run stronger, inspiration flows freely, and game-changing ideas present themselves like low-hanging fruit ripe for the picking. And once these periods have run their course, it's as if some phantom spigot has mysteriously turned off and those brilliant feelings and ideas are suddenly harder to come by. I once heard a yogi remark that the "truly great souls" choose to incarnate onto the Earth at powerful times in history, like the Italian Renaissance or Sophocles' Athens, because of the opportunities those times present. Difficult as that may be to prove, it makes a certain reincarnational sense, when you stop to think about it. By analogy, would a budding world-class gymnast want to attend a strictly average athletic school or prefer to enroll in the best institution available? Likewise, would Albert Einstein be more likely to incarnate into a period that's totally out of sync with his abilities and skills – or one that offers the optimal circumstances for developing his brilliant ideas?

Consider that the hugely successful author, J. K. Rowling, was born precisely as Uranus was conjoining Pluto in 1965 and penned works that sold millions of copies. (Note, too, that the Harry Potter character sports a birthmark on his head resembling a very Uranian lightning bolt!) Likewise, Larry and Andy Wachowski, directors of the successful *Matrix* franchise, were born in 1965 and 1967, respectively, and created a film that reached worldwide audiences. The horoscopes of pop sensations like Taylor Swift and Justin Bieber show strong connections between their personal planets and the Uranus/Neptune conjunction of their era. Singer Bob Dylan was born on the heels of the extraordinary configurations of May, 1941, that we've touched upon earlier in this book. Going back further, we find that J. R. R. Tolkien, author of the *Lord of the Rings* series, was born in 1892, during the epochal conjunction of Pluto and Neptune, as were other influential figures like Paramahansa Yogananda (1893), J. Krishnamurti (1895), and Buckminster Fuller (1895). And consider how both Ludwig von Beethoven and Napoleon Bonaparte were born during an extremely rare grand trine in the 1700s between the three outer planets – Uranus, Neptune, and Pluto. In all of these cases, it's as though these individuals' relationship with the transpersonal planets provided them with a finger on the pulse of those generational streams that defined their era – for better or worse.

Final Thoughts
We've looked at a few of the powerful time-windows that have arisen in our past, and there are countless more besides these. However, while some periods may indeed be more energetic or truly revolutionary than others, it's important to point out that all periods have their own unique qualities and set of possibilities. Every era witnesses the rise of individuals who are preternaturally attuned to the potentials of their time, whether constructively or destructively, with one decade witnessing the rise of Michael Jackson and Mikhail Gorbachev, and another one seeing the ascent of Lady Gaga and Barack Obama – and on it goes.

But in more modest ways, even the most obscure individual is a creature of their particular zeitgeist, their thoughts and drives reflecting the necessities of their given era. Is there any way to tell more precisely how a person is aligned to the zeitgeist? One method is to look at whether you were born close in time to any configuration involving the outer planets. Did you arrive in the midst of Uranus square Saturn? If so, then take a moment to reflect on how your life has been concerned with overturning conventional attitudes or structures. Or were you born when Saturn was conjoining Jupiter? If so, then consider how your life has been involved in grappling with systems of religion, law, or morality.

For that matter, any relationship between a personal planet and the slower-moving ones can offer insights into someone's alignment with the shifting zeitgeist. For example, is your natal Venus conjunct transpersonal Neptune – as it was for singer and songwriter Joni Mitchell (born on November 7, 1943)? If so, then it's possible that your own artistic or romantic values have been attuned to more transpersonal currents of feeling throughout your culture, and in turn to Neptune's smorgasbord of angelic dreams or disappointing illusions. Or was your Mercury aligned at birth with Uranus somehow, as it was for Benjamin Franklin (who had an opposition between these planets)? Then, perhaps look to see how your own individual mind has been attuned to the futuristic and innovative trends of the unfolding zeitgeist.

It's even possible for someone to be attuned to the significant time-windows of the past, long before that person was born. My own Venus is at 7 degrees Gemini, which places it exactly on the zodiacal point where Pluto conjoined Neptune in the early 1890s. Curiously, since I was very young, I've been powerfully drawn to the art and music of that period, to composers like Claude Debussy and symbolist artists like Jean Delville. In his book, *Horoscope for the New Millennium*, astrologer E. Alan Meece argues for the lingering effects of that rare once-every-five-centuries conjunction, showing how the horoscopes of various famous figures from the last few decades connect with that pivotal point in history, from John F. Kennedy to Bob Dylan. In other words, we're not just products of our specific birthday but the energies of overlapping horoscopes extending back through time, like some grand cosmic multilayered cake.

As far as any upcoming planetary configurations are concerned, look to where the emerging patterns will fall in your own chart to better understand how your own life may become entwined with that of the collective. In recent years we've witnessed the effects of a powerful Uranus square to Pluto – the "next phase" of the revolutionary wave of change initiated by the conjunction of these two planets in the 1960s. How did you respond to these turbulent impulses? And what area of your life was impacted the most? Someone with Venus aligned to those particular degrees (roughly 7 to 15 degrees of cardinal signs) may have found those energies stirring up their romantic impulses and/or financial dealings, while someone with Jupiter at that point may have felt it strongest in their shifting religious or ideological beliefs.

Having said that, it's important to realize that though we're all shaped by our times, we're not necessarily confined by them. That's because in a certain sense the zeitgeist is whatever we make of it, in terms of utilizing its resources for either constructive or destructive ends. You can hand some people the most expensive art materials and they'll still manage to create crappy art, while others working with the most meager of materials will still manage to concoct masterpieces. Likewise, a great soul can do wondrous things with the planetary potentials offered by their era, just as a less balanced mind can abuse or squander them. Charlie Chaplin and Adolf Hitler were born just days apart, and both were plugged into much the same generational stream. (The two of them also looked alike, interestingly enough) Yet, one chose to channel his talent for mass influence into great art, while the other steered it toward unprecedented death and destruction. The famed yogi Paramahansa Yogananda once implored students to "rise above the age in which you are born." I'd suggest a slightly different variation, namely: As long as we're right here and right now, why not make the most of it?

Reprinted from *The Mountain Astrologer*, October/November 2011.

14

Monsters, Mystics, and the Collective Unconscious: Planetary Cycles and the Outer Limits of the Zeitgeist

We make our own monsters, then fear them for what they show us about ourselves.

Mike Carey and Peter Gross

Like quite a few other boys from my generation with too much time on their hands, I was fascinated while growing up by all things strange and wonderful, from movie monsters and stories about UFOs to rumors of Neanderthal bodies encased in blocks of ice displayed at state fairs around the country. I even learned there was a name for many of these oddities: "Fortean," after the famed early-20th-century chronicler of anomalies, Charles Fort. But whatever name you called them by, I was hooked. And the stranger they were, the better.

Even from a young age, though, I started noticing how these types of stories seemed to occur in noticeable waves or "flaps." Sometimes months would go by without a single UFO report, ghost story, or even monster movie being talked about, when suddenly a spate of these popped up in a relatively short span. No doubt psychology and sociology would have much to say about the reasons for that, but astrology has reasons of its own, I'd come to learn, while providing me with a host of useful insights into this most unconventional side of history.

In the previous chapter, I explored some of the ways planetary cycles trigger tectonic shifts in society. In this chapter I'll be focusing on some of the more unusual manifestations that arise during these cycles, including not just anomalous and "Fortean" events but also some of society's most iconic monsters, both real and fictional. This much is clear: Whenever the outer planets come together, powerful energies are stirred up in the collective unconscious – and the results can sometimes be as terrifying as they are inspiring.

The Lure of the Exotic

As astrological students of history know, all the planets play a role in shaping the zeitgeist, or "spirit of the age." But it's the interaction of the outer bodies – Uranus, Neptune, and Pluto – that seem to play an especially prominent role in shaping the trends and qualities of historical eras.

For instance, outer-planetary aspects – especially conjunctions – often accompany breakthroughs and innovations in the arts and sciences. We've already seen how the Beatles and Bob Dylan reached their creative peaks exactly as Uranus and Pluto came together in the 1960s, which was also a time when humans first set foot on the Moon. This was a decade of enormous social change and "people power," when ordinary citizens took to the streets to make their opinions known about civil rights, women's liberation, and the Vietnam War, among other things. Such movements are typical of the kinds of changes that unfold under the influence of outer-planetary configurations.

But there is another side to these cycles that's generally overlooked, one which reflects a more unusual dimension of their influence. Having lived through two outer-planet conjunctions in my own lifetime (Uranus–Pluto in the mid '60s and Uranus–Neptune during the early '90s), I became intensely aware during both of these periods of a palpable mood of exoticism wafting through the culture, almost like some mysterious incense, which was accompanied by a heightened fascination with the unconventional and the bizarre. Albert Einstein famously wrote that "the most beautiful experience we can have is the mysterious," and to my mind that could well describe the mood of periods like these, because of the way they usher in a fascination with all things unusual and extra-ordinary.

As an illustration, when Uranus and Neptune came together during the late 1980s and early '90s, the obsession with the mysterious and exotic led to a surge of interest in TV shows dealing with fringe subjects like *The X-Files*, *Sightings*, *Star Trek: The Next Generation*, and David Lynch's classic *Twin Peaks*. This period saw an explosion of interest in the field of "world music," with exotic new sounds filtering into the cultural mindstream via performers like Dead Can Dance, Deep Forest, Enigma, Margareth Menezes, and Enya. This period also witnessed a massive increase of interest in spiritual topics that resulted in a spate of publications and workshops devoted to Eastern religions, shamanism, New Age thought, and Native American practices.

This "call of the wild" extended not just through space but time as well. Having worked in the publishing industry during that period, I was struck by the extraordinary popularity of any and all media projects related to ancient and "lost civilizations" – particularly Egypt and Atlantis. That trend climaxed with two events in particular: first, the 1993 premiere of NBC's Emmy Award–winning prime-time special, *Mystery of the Sphinx*, hosted by Charlton Heston (based on the research of John Anthony West and Robert Schoch); and second, the unveiling of tomb KV5 in Egypt's Valley of the Kings in 1995, the most significant Egyptian burial site discovered since that of King Tut.

Or, turning back the clock to the previous Uranus–Pluto conjunction of the mid '60s, it was as though the public suddenly developed a newfound openness to previously offbeat ideas and genres, as reflected in TV shows like *The Twilight Zone, Outer Limits, Thriller, The Invaders, One Step Beyond*, and the original *Star Trek*. Musically, teenagers like myself were turning on their radios and hearing strange instruments like sitars and tablas now gracing pop songs by the Beatles, Donavan, and the Rolling Stones, while flautist Paul Horn was recording his jazz-influenced melodies in the sublime open spaces of the Taj Mahal. Books on yoga and oriental/alternative spirituality were becoming hugely popular, among them Jess Stearn's *Yoga, Youth, and Reincarnation*; Louis Pauwels' and Jacques Bergier's *Morning of the Magicians;* the collected works of Edgar Cayce; the "ancient astronaut" theories of Erich von Däniken; the faux-Tibetan teachings of Lobsang Rampa; and Linda Goodman's best-selling astrology primer, *Sun Signs*.

Stepping back further to the once-every-five-hundred-year alignment of Pluto and Neptune, during the late 1880s and early '90s, there was a similar explosion of exotic or "fringe" interests taking place then, too, with mystical groups like the Theosophical Society and the Golden Dawn rising to prominence, and the Parliament of World Religions exposing Western audiences to foreign teachings through figures such as Swami Vivekenanda. Composers like Debussy, Rimsky-Korsakov, and Tchaikovsky were incorporating oriental motifs into their music, while symbolist painters like Jean Delville and Odilon Redon were taking their art into increasingly mystical directions, just as art nouveau was infusing art and architecture with its own dreamy influences.

Rolling back the calendar to the previous outer-planet conjunction of Uranus and Neptune, which climaxed in 1821, we see these planets reflected not only in the growing popularity of gothic fiction but also in the extraordinary art of painters like Caspar David Friedrich with his exquisite depictions of mystery and solitude. This period also played host to a truly iconic event in the history of the human imagination: Champollion's translation of ancient Egyptian hieroglyphics in 1822. For students of history and even ordinary citizens at the time, it felt as though the door to a long-lost world of knowledge had suddenly opened, with the promise of great mysteries about to be unveiled. In many ways, this was a period of heightened aspiration and a "yearning for the ineffable," probably best illustrated in 1824 by the "Ode to Joy" in the fourth movement of Beethoven's Ninth Symphony, with lyrics like these:

Brothers, above the starry canopy
Must a loving Father dwell.
Do you bow down, millions?
Do you sense the Creator, world?
Seek Him beyond the starry canopy!
Beyond the stars must He dwell.

The Breaking Open of the Untameable

Examples like these suggest to me that certain periods represent especially dramatic "openings" into the collective unconscious, as though the membrane between worlds thins and allows us to intuit realities and ideas normally beyond our grasp. Some of that is likely due to the way these outer bodies – Uranus, Neptune, and Pluto – represent forces outside the conventional framework defined by Saturn, making them inherently unorthodox and "against the grain" in symbolism.

But I suspect it also stems from the fact that these bodies are so distant from Earth that they're essentially invisible to the naked eye – thus symbolizing forces deep in the collective unconscious. The result is that whenever they're triggered, it feels like tectonic plates shifting deep underground and awakening forces that seem wholly alien or other, as if issued from another world. And in a certain sense, they may well be.

On one level, this manifests as a growing fascination with subjects or phenomena that seem mysterious or distant from us in space or time. Because our intuition is now sensing what lies beyond the veil of surface appearances, we're suddenly attracted to ideas and images that previously seemed bizarre or unconventional.

But it's even possible that such periods produce not only a heightened fascination with the *other*, but also a greater occurrence of unusual or Fortean events in the world. It's as though the veil between worlds doesn't simply become thin but in some sense is actually pierced, allowing for the contents of these alternate realities to bleed through into our world, like a finger being pulled out from the cosmic dike.

Take the Uranus–Neptune conjunction of the late 1980s and early '90s. Throughout that period, there was a growing interest in the phenomenon of EVP – or Electronic Voice Projection – as researchers like Mark Macy and George Meek gained attention for their work on purported communication with the dead via radio and television technology. That same period also saw a massive increase in the popularity of mediumship (rebranded at the time as "channeling"), with a series of books and TV programs flooding the market on messages received from disembodied beings of one ilk or another. The crop circle phenomenon was also exploding into pubic attention during the early 1990s, as skeptics and believers alike debated whether these increasingly complex formations were messages from aliens, time travelers, parallel dimensions, earthbound invisibles, or simply the work of hoaxers. It's probably not a coincidence that the popular film *Stargate* premiered during the peak of this period, in 1994, with its story about a mysterious portal opening up to distant worlds – and in a way it felt just like that at the time!

And going back to the Uranus–Pluto conjunction of the mid 1960s, this was a decade that witnessed a massive influx of anomalous reports filtering in through the mainstream media, from sightings of UFOs in places like Michigan and Shag Harbour to the iconic filming of an alleged Bigfoot in California in October 1967. The mid '60s also played host to one of the most bizarre anomalies of recent times, the Mothman sightings of West Virginia, commencing in 1966 and climaxing with the deadly collapse of the Silver Bridge on September 15, 1967 in that same area.

Seven decades earlier, the 1890s were also an active time for Fortean-style incidents, best exemplified by the great "airship wave" of 1896–97, when mysterious floating craft were reported by witnesses around the United States, as well as the pre-Roswell claim of a crashed spaceship in Aurora, Texas in 1897.

In his classic work, *The Varieties of Religious Experience*, American philosopher William James pointed out:

> Our normal waking consciousness, rational consciousness as we call it, is but one special type of consciousness, whilst all about it, parted from it by the filmiest of screens, there lie potential forms of consciousness entirely different.

If even a fraction of the Fortean accounts passed down to us represent real events, then it's possible that that "filmiest of screens" James described might open wide at certain points, allowing for a true cross-pollination of dimensions to take place.

Angels and Demons

Wherever God erects a house of prayer, the devil builds a chapel.

Daniel Defoe

With every opening up of the collective unconscious comes a certain trade-off, since this piercing of the veil affords contact not just with the lighter and more spiritual aspects of consciousness but its darker potentials as well. Consequently, with the entrance of powerful divine energies into our world, we also find the emergence of powerful negative forces. Time after time, while studying the historical records, I was struck by how often the activation of the outer planets coincided with the emergence of not only great or unusual manifestations but also society's most notable monsters, both fictional and real.

As a case in point, the Uranus–Neptune conjunction of the early 1990s may well have triggered a spiritual renaissance, in terms of books, journals, and teachings, but it also witnessed a milestone in cinematic monster-making with the release of Steven Spielberg's *Jurassic Park* (premiering in 1993, the very year that planetary conjunction became exact). The same year, Spielberg gave us another film dealing with monsters of the Nazi variety, with his movie *Schindler's List*. On the real-world stage, this period also saw the eruption of unspeakable horrors in regions of the world like Rwanda, Bosnia, Sierra Leone, and Iraq.

Rewinding to the Uranus–Pluto conjunction of the 1960s, this decade witnessed advances in areas like civil rights, science, and the arts, but it also saw the box-office popularity of the Japanese monster franchise headlined by creatures like *Godzilla*, *Gamera*, *Ghidora*, *Guiron*, and *Mothra*, and God-knows-what other weirdly named creatures from the Tokyo studios. The '60s were also a high-water mark in stop-motion special effects monsters, through the work of Ray Harryhausen in films like *Jason and the Argonauts*, *From the Earth to the Moon*, and *Mysterious Island*. In real life, this decade saw horrendous violence in the Vietnam War as well as China's Cultural Revolution. And just as the peace-and-love festival of Woodstock was followed several months later by the violence-plagued Altamont concert, so too the largely positive message of the Beatles found its dark counterpoint in the crimes of the Manson family; the two groups even shared a common tagline: "Helter Skelter."

Reflecting back on the Neptune–Pluto conjunction of the late 1800s, this may have been a period rich in mystical, creative, and technological trends, but it was also a time that introduced us to Bram Stoker's *Dracula* (1897), Arthur Machen's seminal horror novel, *The Great God Pan* (1894), and the real-life monster Jack the Ripper. And let's not forget that the 1890s gave birth to history's first horror film, Georges Méliès' *Le Manoir du diable*.

And stepping back earlier to the Uranus–Neptune conjunction of the early 1820s, the same period that gave us Beethoven's Ninth and the decoding of ancient Egyptian hieroglyphics also gave birth to that other great icon of modern horror – Mary Shelley's *Frankenstein* (published anonymously in 1818 and then republished under Shelley's name in the 1823 second edition).

The Lessons of Monsters
So, what can we learn from these monstrous apparitions, whether real or fictional? In much the same way that the creatures of our personal nightmares reveal truths and lessons we need to face within ourselves, I believe the monsters of our collective dreams hold a similar significance. They embody, in exaggerated form, the titanic energies of our own psyches and the lessons we're struggling to learn as a society.

For instance, it's fitting that Mary Shelley's story of a mechanical monster should appear exactly in the wake of the Industrial Revolution, when more sensitive minds were re-examining the fruits of technological progress, not to mention mechanistic rationality itself. Similarly, Bram Stoker's *Dracula* expressed something appropriate to the darker qualities of *fin de siècle* 19th-century Europe, this being a period not just of mystical and spiritual fascinations but widespread drug epidemics, "decadence," and late-Romantic escapism.

Or consider the atomic-generated monsters of Japanese cinema during the 1950s and '60s, an era when people around the planet were gripped by fears of nuclear holocaust and the lingering effects of atomic radiation.

What about the monsters populating our collective dreams now? Though I've been focusing my attention here mainly on conjunctions between the outer planets, the fact is that any strong relationship between the outer bodies can trigger powerful openings into the collective unconscious. For instance, the Uranus–Pluto square of the early 1850s saw the publication of one of literature's towering achievements, Herman Melville's *Moby Dick*, which simultaneously introduced us to one of the most iconic fictional monsters – Ahab's great white whale.

And on March 2, 1933, one of Hollywood's most enduring monster movies, *King Kong*, premiered exactly as Pluto and Uranus were within only minutes of arc from an exact square (a 90-degree angle). That planetary conflict was reflected in the symbolism of the final battle between Kong (Pluto) and the fighter planes (Uranus). It's worth noting that, in Germany, this same month saw full dictatorial powers being acquired by Adolf Hitler (due to passage of the Enabling Act), whose army was eventually taken down, in large part by enemy planes.

As of this writing (summer 2013), the world is in the midst of another series of squares between Uranus and Pluto. A number of "monsters" populate the global landscape now, from the political tyrants of nations like Syria and North Korea to corporate tyrants like Monsanto and the Bank of America. In cinema, the summer of 2013 has seen the release of Guillermo del Toro's big-budget film, *Pacific Rim*, which revolves around a gigantic, scientifically engineered robot doing battle with a monstrous beast from the underworld. Could there be a more fitting expression of Uranus in conflict with Pluto, I wonder? Symbolically viewed, there's a close correspondence between the film's narrative and what has been unfolding on the global stage: on the one hand, the film's Uranian hi-tech robot aptly signifies the rise of progressive, even futuristic attitudes, while the film's primeval beast symbolizes comparatively regressive, reptile-brain forces in the world seeking to control others or maintain the status quo – or both.

The battle between these titanic figures reflects the struggle taking place now between new and old, between future and past, as the emerging Aquarian paradigm struggles to overcome resistance from traditional institutions and entrenched values. Think of Occupy Wall Street vs. Wall Street, the Arab Spring vs. Middle Eastern dictators, the Syrian rebels vs. President Assad, conflicts like the Tea Party vs. the U.S. federal government, or the "New Atheists" vs. traditional religion. One way or another, these all reflect the underlying conflict in our each of psyches throughout this planetary phase.[1]

Final Thoughts

As we've seen, when the outer planets interact and the portal to the collective unconscious opens up, powerful energies flow into manifestation in ways that can affect the course of history for years to come, giving rise not only to creative achievements but horrific forces as well. Yet, precisely because these energies can be channeled in either positive or negative ways, the very magnitude of the monsters appearing during these periods speaks to the magnitude of the creative and spiritual possibilities available during these times, too. The poet Ogden Nash once wrote, "Where there is a monster, there is a miracle." Look back to any of the eras recounted above, for instance, and you'll see a striking symmetry between the "good" and "bad" developments taking shape at each turn of the wheel.

Just think back to the 20th century's most iconic real-life "monster," Adolf Hitler, who was born just as the epic Neptune–Pluto conjunction was gaining momentum during the late 1880s. That very same week also saw the birth of one of history's great comedic and artistic geniuses, Charlie Chaplin (who looked virtually identical to his German counterpart). Examples like this remind me of what physicists describe, using their own language – that one can't create matter without also creating its opposite in antimatter. In a sense, angels and demons come in pairs, never alone.

Holding that in mind, it's worth reflecting on what the monsters of our own time could be telling us about the possibilities available to us now. While it's far too early to know the full impact of the recent Uranus–Pluto square, we already see signs of important shifts taking place in areas like gay rights, '60s-style "people power," environmental awareness, and science in general. Physicists have announced that they've finally discovered the long-theorized Higgs boson, or "God particle," and in recent months some researchers have even claimed to have found evidence for the existence of universes besides our own!

Remember, too, that the spectrum of extremes we see manifesting on the collective level during such configurations applies to us as individuals, too. In other words, the enormous potentials for good or ill associated with strong aspects between Uranus, Neptune, or Pluto are every bit as present in the lives of personalities born under these aspects. I already mentioned how Chaplin and Hitler reflected the highs and lows of the Neptune–Pluto influence, at one point during the late 19th century, but we could also add some of the figures born under the Uranus–Pluto square of the early 1930s to this list. True, this period gave birth to sociopaths like Charles Manson, Jim Jones, and Marshall Applewhite, but it also ushered in creative spirits like Leonard Cohen, Carl Sagan, and Elvis Presley.

That's worth keeping in mind when attempting to fathom the meaning and impact of the Uranus–Pluto square that's been convulsing the world in recent years. What will be the final legacy of this period and its wildly turbulent energies? The truth is, we may not know the answer until the children born under its influence have grown up and made their own mark on the world – for better or worse!

Note
1. My thanks to Dave Gunning for his feedback on this passage.

Reprinted from *The Mountain Astrologer*, February/March 2014.

15

Tectonic Triggers:
The Hidden Power of Station Points

Have you ever looked at someone's horoscope and felt puzzled by the discrepancy between the planetary energy expressed in their personality and what was suggested by their charts? For instance, a person with a heavily Saturnian chart but who exhibits an unusually Jupiterian personality? Or someone with a confident-looking horoscope who acts relatively timid in person?

There are any number of possible reasons for discrepancies like that – overlooked declinations, alternate systems of measurement (such as vedic or hellenistic), or simple misinterpretation. But one factor I've sometimes found to be responsible involves what astrologers call the *station point*. Look up that term in any basic astrology source and it will usually say that it's when a planet slows down and stands relatively still before changing directions, and either starts going backward ("retrograde") or forward ("direct"). Think "station" as in *stationary*, in other words.

But while many astrologers look to the station point primarily for what it tells us about when and where a planet is changing direction, stations possess another level of meaning that's often overlooked, and which could be even more important in symbolism than its role as a directional marker. Why? Because in the process of slowing down and grinding to a seeming halt, the influence of that planet is dramatically amplified, creating what one early teacher of mine called a "branding iron" effect.[1] To use a simple analogy, imagine you're walking very quickly across a surface of freshly poured cement. You'll make impressions on that surface, no doubt, but they probably won't go deep. But if you were to stop midway across that surface and stand motionless for a minute or two, your feet would sink considerably deeper, making a more noticeable impression.

Station points are like that. Because a planet occupies one spot in the zodiac for a longer period, it has the chance to make a deeper impression on your horoscope than it normally would. Just as importantly, not only will that planet's energy be amplified, but *any aspect it forms to other planets will be, too*. Grasping this simple fact can hold dramatic implications for our astrological practice, and has led me to believe that station points are among the most significant –

but overlooked – tools of our trade. What I'll be doing in this chapter is examining some of the implications of station points for both personal charts as well as mundane, socio-cultural horoscopes, as well as for prediction. To begin with, let's look at their role in the natal horoscope.

Station Points in the Natal Horoscopes

When looking at charts, many astrologers will naturally check to see whether a planet is retrograde or direct, but comparatively few stop to examine whether that planet falls within the broader span of its station, or what might be called the "stationary zone" – those days on either side of that shift in direction when the planet is comparatively motionless. Much of the reason for that oversight is no doubt due to the fact that modern computers perform most of the calculations for us nowadays, thus eliminating the need to even open up an ephemeris – a simple act that would quickly reveal whether or not a planet falls within a stationary period.[2]

Of course, many of the horoscopes you study might not include any planets directly within the penumbra of a stationary period. But when they do, it can provide added clarity and insight into individual's lives. Consider the case of inventor Nikola Tesla, who famously displayed extraordinary intuition into the hidden laws of nature. His understanding of electricity and other "invisible" forces was so profound he's come to be regarded by some as almost more of a mystic than a scientist. Born on July 10, 1856, in Smiljan, Croatia (0.00 AM LMT) his chart shows that Neptune was at 20 degrees of Pisces, and was trining his Sun, widely squaring Mercury, and forming a sextile to Uranus in his 1st house. Together, these factors show an intuitive and imaginative personality – but not necessarily anything extraordinary.

But when we open up the ephemeris for July 10, 1856, we see that when he was born, Neptune was stationary and occupied the same zodiacal degree from May 13 all the way up through August 4 of that year (and occupied the same *exact degree and minute* from June 21 to 25). In short, Tesla was born well within the influence of the Neptune station. This amplifies the importance of his natal Neptune considerably, along with its associated aspects. Little wonder he had such an intuitive mind regarding nature's energetic forces (note the sextile to 1st house Uranus in Taurus) – just as it's also little wonder he also experienced bitter disappointments in his business dealings with colleagues like Thomas Edison (Tesla's Neptune squaring Mercury)![3]

GMT +0:00 Tropical Geocentric Long	Uranus ♅	Neptune ♆	Pluto ♇
1 Jul 1856 NS	23° ♉ 34'	20° ♓ 26' ℞	05° ♉ 27'
2 Jul 1856 NS	23° ♉ 36'	20° ♓ 25'	05° ♉ 28'
3 Jul 1856 NS	23° ♉ 39'	20° ♓ 25'	05° ♉ 28'
4 Jul 1856 NS	23° ♉ 42'	20° ♓ 25'	05° ♉ 29'
5 Jul 1856 NS	23° ♉ 44'	20° ♓ 24'	05° ♉ 30'
6 Jul 1856 NS	23° ♉ 47'	20° ♓ 24'	05° ♉ 30'
7 Jul 1856 NS	23° ♉ 49'	20° ♓ 23'	05° ♉ 31'
8 Jul 1856 NS	23° ♉ 52'	20° ♓ 23'	05° ♉ 31'
9 Jul 1856 NS	23° ♉ 54'	20° ♓ 22'	05° ♉ 32'
10 Jul 1856 NS	23° ♉ 56'	20° ♓ 22'	05° ♉ 33'
11 Jul 1856 NS	23° ♉ 59'	20° ♓ 21'	05° ♉ 33'
12 Jul 1856 NS	24° ♉ 01'	20° ♓ 21'	05° ♉ 34'
13 Jul 1856 NS	24° ♉ 03'	20° ♓ 20'	05° ♉ 34'
14 Jul 1856 NS	24° ♉ 06'	20° ♓ 20'	05° ♉ 35'
15 Jul 1856 NS	24° ♉ 08'	20° ♓ 19'	05° ♉ 35'
16 Jul 1856 NS	24° ♉ 10'	20° ♓ 18'	05° ♉ 35'
17 Jul 1856 NS	24° ♉ 12'	20° ♓ 17'	05° ♉ 36'
18 Jul 1856 NS	24° ♉ 14'	20° ♓ 17'	05° ♉ 36'
19 Jul 1856 NS	24° ♉ 16'	20° ♓ 16'	05° ♉ 37'

With these points in mind, let's take a look at some cases of well-known individuals born during planetary stations, using examples for each of the major planetary bodies (remembering, of course, that the Sun and the Moon never go retrograde). An important note: in the case of faster moving bodies like Mercury or Venus, a planet will slow down and occupy the same zodiacal space for only a few days, while in the case of slower moving bodies like Pluto, a planet can remain in the same basic degree for a month or two on either side of its directional shift – and can occupy the *same exact degree and minute* for seven or eight days straight. As a result, I naturally allow a wider berth for the date-boundaries of outer planet stations than for those of the faster-moving bodies. With that said, let us begin.

Mercury Station
Individuals born during these periods display a heightened emphasis on the mind and communication, with the zodiacal sign involved providing further clues into its expression.

- Welsh poet Dylan Thomas was born on October 27, 1914, exactly as Mercury was stationary in Scorpio, while the American poet John Berryman was born two days earlier, also within the influence of the Mercury station.

- Hillary Clinton was born on October 26, 1947, when Mercury was stationary in Scorpio, having gone retrograde just one day earlier.

- Straight-talking media commentator, Chris Matthews, was born on December 17, 1945 exactly as Mercury was stationing in Sagittarius.

- Soviet dictator Joseph Stalin was born on December 18, 1878, just as Mercury was stationing in strategic Capricorn, having turned retrograde just one day earlier.

- Archetypal psychologist James Hillman was born on April 12, 1926, with Mercury stationary in Aries, turning direct the next day.

- Filmmaker and businessman George Lucas was born on May 14, 1944, exactly as Mercury was stationing in Taurus, turning direct the next day.

Venus Station

Individuals born during a Venus station often display a pronounced interest in the arts, an appreciation of worldly pleasures, or a love of social interactions throughout their lives.

- Actor, producer, and off-screen lothario Warren Beatty was born on March 30, 1937, while retrograde Venus was stationing in its own sign of Taurus.

- Actor Robert De Niro was born on August 17, 1943, two days after Venus went retrograde in Virgo.

- Singer Chaka Khan was born on March 23, 1953, during a double-header station of Venus and Uranus.

- Singer Amy Winehouse was born on September 14, 1983, during a double station of Venus and Neptune.

- Renaissance artist and sculptor Michelangelo was born on March 6, 1475 exactly during a station of Venus in Aries, turning retrograde the next day. Saturn was also nearly motionless as well, turning direct on March 10.

Mars Station

Individuals born during a Mars station can exhibit a sense of power or assertiveness in their personalities, and sometimes a quality of sexual magnetism. If stressfully aspected, there may be issues with anger or power struggles in their personal or professional lives.

- Led Zeppelin guitarist and occult aficionado Jimmy Page was born on January 9, 1944, during a double station of both Mars and Neptune.

- Latina actress Chita Rivera, was born on January 23, 1933, while Mars was stationary.

- Powerhouse soul singer Otis Redding was born on September 9, 1941, during a triple station of Mars, Uranus, and Saturn.

- Wartime president Franklin Delano Roosevelt was born on January 30, 1882, while Mars was stationing in Gemini, prominently situated near his Midheaven.

- Writer James Joyce was born three days later on February 2, 1882, the same day Mars went direct in communicative Gemini.

- U.S. Presidential candidate Bernie Sanders was born on September 8, 1941, during a triple station of Mars, Uranus, and Saturn.

- Media mogul Rupert Murdoch was born on March 11, 1931, during a double station of both Mars and Jupiter in acquisitive Cancer.

- Psychologist Carl Jung was born on July 26, 1875, during a station of Mars in Sagittarius, which turned direct one day earlier.

Jupiter Station

Being born under a Jupiter station can manifest as a more religious or ideological inclination, or simply as a more expansive vision in one's work or personal life.

- The Dalai Lama was born on July 6, 1935, under the influence of a Jupiter station in Scorpio.

- Businessman Donald (Bigger is better!) Trump was born on June 14, 1946, during a double station of Jupiter and Neptune.

- Adolph Hitler was born on April 20, 1889, in the midst of a Jupiter station in Capricorn. Hitler's political aspirations were nothing if not expansive; hailing from a commoner's background, his goals included nothing less than conquering the entire planet and creating a "Third Reich" that would last a thousand years.

- Controversial religious leader Louis Farrakhan (birth name Louis Eugene Wolcott) was born on May 11, 1933, exactly as Jupiter was stationing in Virgo, conjuncting Neptune and trining the Sun.[4]

- Actor Tom Cruise was born on July 3, 1962, just as a tightly stationing Jupiter amplified an already expansive grand trine to Neptune and the Sun.

- Essayist and poet Ralph Waldo Emerson was born on May 25, 1803, the day after Jupiter turned direct in Virgo.

- Singer Paul Simon was born on October 13, 1941, during a double station of Jupiter and Mercury.

- Marlon Brando was born on April 3, 1924, during a station of Jupiter in Sagittarius.

Saturn Station

Individuals born during Saturn stations are often notable for their tenacity and discipline, and can be "late bloomers" in their professional or emotional lives. There is sometimes an underlying heaviness to their personalities, as if they're bearing a heavy weight, but they can also reveal surprising depth.

- Dick Cavett was born on November 19, 1936, the same day Saturn went direct in Pisces, while opposing Neptune in Virgo. Despite gaining acclaim both as a comedian and talk show host, Cavett confessed in later years to a lifelong struggle with depression.

- TV commentator, social advocate, and former White House consultant Bill Moyers was born on June 5, 1934, during a double station of Saturn and Jupiter.

- Actor Liam Neeson, whose stage persona one critic described as that of "somber gravitas," was born on June 7, 1952, exactly during a double station of both Saturn and Mars. It's perhaps fitting that Neeson gained his greatest box-office success as an aging action hero in his sixties, as the lead in the hugely successful *Taken* franchise!

- Actress Gillian Anderson (agent Scully of *The X-Files*) was born on August 9, 1968, during a double station of skeptical Saturn and mystical Neptune.

- Saturn can bring great success and achievement – but sometimes great falls from grace, too, as evidenced by these two examples: comedian Bill Cosby, was born on July 12, 1937 during a station of Saturn in Aries (the zodiacal sign associated with assertiveness and drive); and disgraced cyclist Lance Armstrong, who was born on September 18, 1971, just one day before Saturn turned retrograde in Gemini (the zodiacal sign associated with short-distance travel).

Uranus Station

Those born under the influence of stationing Uranus can be independent with a strong concern for personal freedom and self-expression. Depending on aspects to personal planets or horoscopic placements, they may be interested in social reform and progressive social change or, at the other extreme, behave like 'free agents' who selfishly follow their own rules without regard for others.

- President Abraham Lincoln was born on February 12, 1809, the same day Uranus reversed directions while trining Mercury and Pluto.

- Famed biologist Charles Darwin was born on the same day as Lincoln, and sparked a cultural revolution in both scientific and religious circles with his theories of evolution.

- President John F. Kennedy was born on May 29, 1917, during a double station of Uranus in Aquarius and Mercury in Taurus (with both forming a square to one another).

- Napoleon Bonaparte was born on August 15, 1769, just one day before stationing Uranus went direct in Taurus – amplifying an extremely rare grand trine between the outer three planets.

- Singer and musician (Nine Inch Nails) Trent Reznor was born on May 17, 1965, exactly as Uranus was stationing in Virgo (while conjuncting Pluto, opposing Saturn, and squaring Venus/Jupiter in Gemini).

- Shock-rock singer Marilyn Manson (real name Brian Hugh Warner) was born on January 5, 1969, while stationing Uranus was conjunct Jupiter and trining Mercury.

- Pop singer Lady Gaga was born on March 28, 1986, while Uranus was stationing in Sagittarius and trining Venus and squaring Mercury.

- Multimedia superstar Elvis Presley was born on January 8, 1935, during a station of Uranus in Aries, which was the focal point of a multiplanet T-square involving Pluto, Mercury, Venus and the Sun.

- Filmmaker and TV personality Alfred Hitchcock was born on August 13, 1899, while a stationing Uranus was forming a grand trine to his Ascendant and Midheaven.

- Vice President Dick Cheney was born on January 30, 1941, while Uranus was stationing in Taurus near his Midheaven. Though a staunch conservative, Cheney acquired a reputation amongst both friends and foes as a 'lone wolf' who went his own way on matters of business and politics.

Neptune Station

Depending on aspects to personal planets or horoscopic placements, those born under the influence of a Neptune station may show special sensitivity towards the arts, spirituality, or humanitarian concerns – or more negatively, a susceptibility to escapism, self-delusion, or messianic tendencies.

- Bhagwan Shree Rajneesh (also known as "Osho") was born on December 11, 1931, during a triple station of Neptune, Jupiter, and Mercury.

- Jim Jones of "Jonestown" infamy was born on May 13, 1931, during a double station of Mercury and Neptune (with the latter planet trining Mercury and his Ascendant).

- Just four days later, Marshall Applewhite was born on May 17, under the influence of the same Neptune station point (which was still trining Mercury but now also forming a square to the Sun).

- Film director (*The Sixth Sense*) M. Night Shyamalan was born on August 6, 1970, while Neptune was stationing in Scorpio and opposing Saturn in Taurus.

- Singer Rod Stewart was born on January 10, 1945, during a double station of Neptune and Jupiter (the latter trining his Capricorn Sun).

- Writer J. K. Rowling was born on July 31, 1965, during a station of Neptune in Scorpio.

Pluto Station

Depending on aspects to personal planets or horoscopic placements, individuals born under the influence of Pluto approach their lives with a sense of both passion and will, qualities that can either lift them to the heights of creativity and spiritual achievement or plummet them into depths of anger or despair.

- Singer Neil Young was born on November 12, 1945, one day before Pluto turned retrograde, while squaring his Sun and Ascendant, opposing his Moon, and trining his Mercury.

- Young's fellow Canadian Scorpio, Joni Mitchell, was born on November 7, 1943, while stationing Pluto was squaring her Sun and Mercury, and sextiling her Uranus and Neptune. (Joni's friend and colleague, playright and actor Sam Shepard, was born two days earlier on November 5, 1943, under the same Pluto station.)

- Norwegian adventurer (the "Kon Tiki" expeditions) Thor Hayerdahl was born on October 6, 1914, during a double station of Pluto and Jupiter.

- Star of the hit TV series 24, Kiefer Sutherland was born on December 21, 1966, exactly as Pluto was stationing.

- Visionary artist Alex Grey was born on November 29th, 1953, while Pluto was stationing and forming a square to Venus and sextiling Neptune and Jupiter.

- When composer Johann Sebastian Bach was born on March 31, 1685, Pluto was stationary and forming a close trine to Venus and Mercury, while squaring his Sun, Ascendant and Jupiter.[5]

- A musician of a very different sort, Bill Wyman of the Rolling Stones was born on October 24, 1936, while a stationing Pluto was forming a square to his Scorpio Sun and a trine to his Venus.[6]

The Role of Station Points in Prediction

One of the major challenges for any predictively-oriented astrologer is being able to pinpoint not just the meaning of an emerging pattern but its timing. If one's approach to prediction chiefly involves working with transits, that usually includes looking at the dates when those aspects are exact by degree, or what some call *partile*.

But station points can play a pivotal role in refining these interpretations. For instance, suppose Saturn is squaring a client's natal Sun over the course of a given year. The ephemeris or computerized 'hit-list' might show that this square will be exact three times during that year. But as often as not, you'll discover that the most important manifestations of that aspect won't occur when the aspect is exact, but at other times before, during, or after those precise dates. That's because the Sun/Saturn square can be triggered along the way by other, secondary factors, such as eclipses, transits from the other planets – or, as we'll now see, station points.

For instance, over the course of that client's year, Saturn will be stationary at various times while crossing over that exact square point, inching a little ahead or behind each time. *Every one of those stationary periods will activate that Saturn/Sun square in a powerful way.* As a result, what might have seemed at first glance to be three exact trigger points can actually prove to be five or even more triggers (especially if one includes the station points on either side of that square zone). In short, rather than simply noting the key times when the transit is exact, it's vital to pay attention to the station points associated with that *entire period*. Each one will provide further clues into the unfolding drama represented by that transit.

Along with that, station points can also play a role in what I call the "sneak preview" effect, by providing us with an early glimpse into impending trends long before they happen. To illustrate this, let's remain with our example of the client experiencing a transiting Saturn squaring their Sun. Long before that aspect becomes exact, Saturn will have slowly inched forward and backward through the zodiac, like the ebb and flow of a tide, while making its way towards the partile point. Every time it stops to change directions, those station points will activate that impending square, and thus serve as early 'windows' into what will likely happen more fully later on. In the case of our Saturn/Sun client, they could start seeing problems crop up at work, such as difficulties with their boss or an increased workload. If so, that will suggest that the exact square further down the road will likewise be work-related – or possibly even indicate a danger of getting fired or laid-off. Armed with that knowledge, the client can take necessary precautions by being more careful on the job – or even making contingency plans for alternate employment possibilities.

Station Points and Mundane Astrology

At the start of this chapter I asked whether you've ever had the experience of looking at someone's chart and were mystified by the seeming discrepancy between their personality and what was indicated by their horoscope. Now I'd like to pose a similar question, but in relation to mundane astrology: Have you ever studied a historic event or development where the horoscope for that event didn't quite seem to explain it, or account for its magnitude?

As with personal horoscopes, such discrepancies can be due to a variety of things – such as the delayed influence of prior stelliums and eclipses, transits to a nation's horoscope, or yet undiscovered planets. But in some cases, I've found that the precipitating cause for an event may lie in a powerful station point. As an example, consider one of the most dramatic and widely discussed events of the classical world – the assassination of Julius Caesar, on March 15, 44 BCE. The transits for that day were interesting in their own way – most notably, we find a T-square to Saturn which involved Pluto, the Sun and Mercury. But as important a configuration as that may be, it's not an exceptionally rare one, nor does it manifest as the death of a great leader every time it comes around.

Yet when we look at the ephemeris for March 15 of that year, we discover that Pluto was in the midst of a major station point. This is notable for a few reasons. For one, it served to amplify the energy of Pluto far beyond the norm, and along with it, the archetypal motifs of death, secretive actions, power struggles, and transformation. But just as importantly, the station simultaneously amplified the force of the T-square it was involved with – thus taking a dramatic planetary pattern and making it into something truly historic.

151

GMT +0:00 Tropical Geocentric Long	Uranus ♅	Neptune ♆	Pluto ♇
8 Mar 0044 BC	27°♍03' ℞	12°♌13' ℞	29°♊20' ℞
9 Mar 0044 BC	27°♍00'	12°♌11'	29°♊20'
10 Mar 0044 BC	26°♍58'	12°♌10'	29°♊20'
11 Mar 0044 BC	26°♍55'	12°♌09'	29°♊20'
12 Mar 0044 BC	26°♍53'	12°♌07'	29°♊20'
13 Mar 0044 BC	26°♍50'	12°♌06'	29°♊20'
14 Mar 0044 BC	26°♍48'	12°♌05'	29°♊20'
15 Mar 0044 BC	26°♍45'	12°♌04'	29°♊20'
16 Mar 0044 BC	26°♍42'	12°♌03'	29°♊20' D
17 Mar 0044 BC	26°♍40'	12°♌01'	29°♊20'
18 Mar 0044 BC	26°♍37'	12°♌00'	29°♊20'
19 Mar 0044 BC	26°♍35'	11°♌59'	29°♊20'
20 Mar 0044 BC	26°♍32'	11°♌58'	29°♊20'
21 Mar 0044 BC	26°♍30'	11°♌57'	29°♊20'
22 Mar 0044 BC	26°♍27'	11°♌56'	29°♊20'
23 Mar 0044 BC	26°♍25'	11°♌55'	29°♊20'
24 Mar 0044 BC	26°♍22'	11°♌54'	29°♊21'

Station points like this are important for yet another reason. When a planet changes direction – particularly one of the outer, slow-moving bodies – it's akin to the shifting of tectonic plates deep in the collective unconscious. Time and again, one finds station points illuminating historic developments in ways that aren't immediately obvious from examining 'snapshot horoscopes' drawn up for singular moments in time. As with the study of personal horoscopes, looking at an actual ephemeris page sometimes offers advantages over the computer-generated chart, since it can reveal at a glance whether an event falls within a planet's stationary zone.

Battles, Wartime Milestones

With that as a starting point, let's begin by focusing our attention on historic events that appear especially dramatic or explosive in nature, to see whether they occurred in proximity to significant planetary stations. Below are some of the major battles or wartime developments I found that illustrate this. (Note: as I mentioned earlier, stationary periods for the outer planets extend considerably farther out than those of faster-moving bodies like Mercury and Venus, so I've naturally given a wider berth to those in terms of their span on the calendar.)

- British General Charles Cornwallis surrendered at Yorktown on October 19, 1781, an event regarded as the decisive turning point for

American forces in the Revolutionary War. At the time, Pluto was stationing.

- Allied soldiers stormed the beaches at Normandy on June 6, 1944, the same day Neptune changed direction – a fitting connection, considering how closely the attack was not only associated with ocean-based forces but with strategic misdirection by the allies of German intelligence.

- The Siege of Leningrad during World War II took place on September 8, 1941, during a triple station of Mars, Uranus and Saturn. (P.S. As pointed out earlier, note that this was also the date U.S. presidential candidate Bernie Sanders was born!)

- The Cuban Missile Crisis formally came to an end on October 28, 1962. When Jupiter turned direct the very next day, it was as if the entire world breathed a collective sigh of relief over having averted a global nuclear holocaust (something I remember from my own childhood.).

- A tragic milestone in American history was the "Wounded Knee" incident on December 29, 1890, when roughly 300 men, women, and children were slaughtered by U.S. soldiers – an event regarded by many as the symbolic climax of the conflict between Native American tribes and the U.S. government. This event occurred during a station of Saturn.

Political Crises and Scandals

- The Watergate scandal began on June 17, 1972, as triggered by the arrests of the so-called "plumbers" at the Watergate hotel in Washington D.C. Pluto was stationing at the time.

- The first of the Pentagon Papers was published in the New York Times on June 13, 1971, between two stations of Uranus (media) and Pluto (hidden secrets). The documents had a catalyzing effect on the protest movement at the time, by revealing closely guarded information about American military operations in Vietnam.

- Documents obtained by Edward Snowden exposing secret NSA surveillance programs were first released on June 5, 2013, during a station of Neptune in Pisces. (It was exactly during a later station of Neptune, on June 12 of 2015, that media sources published reports how Snowden's stolen documents may have led to breaches of U.S. security by China and Russia, as a result of their decrypting NSA documents leaked by Snowden.)

- From September 9 to 13, 1971, New York was rocked by deadly riots at Attica Prison, resulting in 43 deaths. This took place exactly during a Mars station, followed several days later by Saturn turning direct.

- Robert F. Kennedy was assassinated on June 5, 1968, during a double station of Uranus and Mercury.

- Abraham Lincoln was assassinated on April 14, 1865, under the double station of Venus and Jupiter – a seemingly odd planetary pairing, though it makes sense in light of the outpouring of love for Lincoln amongst supporters following his death, not to mention the jubilation amongst his detractors south of the Mason/Dixon line!

- Mahatma Gandhi's nephew, Rajiv Gandhi, was assassinated on May 17, 1991, on the same day that Saturn went retrograde in Aquarius.

Disasters, Tragedies

- On December 15, 1967, the Silver Bridge in West Virginia collapsed and killed 46 people – an event made famous in connection with the so-called "Mothman" mystery. Three planets were nearly motionless when this happened: Saturn, Jupiter, and Pluto.

- The stock market crash on "Black Friday," October 29, 1929, took place as Pluto was still at a near-crawl, having turned retrograde on October 21.

- On November 20, 1936, a levee failure in Kazuno, Japan resulted in the deaths of 375 people – this occurred exactly as Saturn was stationing in watery Pisces.

- It's especially significant when two or more outer planets experience their stations close to one another, and one such convergence took place during the third week of July 2014, when Uranus and Saturn stationed just three days apart. Among other things, it's important to note that these two planets have long been associated with aviation disasters – including history's deadliest: the Tenerife airport disaster in the Canary Islands, when two planes collided on a runway and killed 583 passengers, just as Saturn and Uranus were locked in a nearly exact square. During the double planetary station of July 2014, the following dramatic events unfolded: Malaysia Airlines Flight 17 was shot down in eastern Ukraine, killing all 298 passengers; two Ukrainian fighter jets were shot down; a Taiwanese jet crashed; an Algerian passenger jet was reported missing; the Israeli/Palestinian conflict heated up dramatically, and some media commentators even began comparing the events of that week to those which ignited World War I, due to reawakened tensions between Putin's Russia and the United States.

Cultural Breakthroughs, Discoveries, and Turning Points

From there I started focusing my attention more on developments concerned more with breakthroughs or advances in culture – technologically, archeologically, scientifically. Among the interesting correlations that came up were these:

- On May 25, 1961, President Kennedy's historic announcement about sending a man to the Moon took place on the same day that Jupiter changed direction in futuristic Aquarius.

- In its own way, NASA's Apollo 8 was almost as much of a watershed event as Apollo 11's Moon mission seven months later, since it was the first time ever that humans broke free of Earth's orbit (raising nightmarish concerns amongst many over the men's fates, had anything gone wrong); this was also the mission when astronauts took the now-iconic photos of the Earth seen from a great distance. The journey lasted from December 21 to 27, 1968, with Pluto turning retrograde on the final day of the mission.

- On May 27, 1937, the same day that Neptune turned direct, the Golden Gate Bridge formally opened to the public – a structure associated not only with scenic photographic vistas but with numerous suicides.

- When Prohibition was formally repealed in the U.S. on December 5, 1933, with the ratification of the Twenty-first Amendment, Neptune was grinding to a halt (finally going retrograde on December 15).

- The Parliament of World Religions in Chicago was a watershed moment in the global exchange of religious ideas, and lasted from September 11 to 27, 1893. At the time there were three major stations occurring – Pluto, Neptune, and Jupiter.

- The most successful sex reassignment surgery prior to recent years was performed in Sweden on November 20, 1952, for Christine Jørgensen during a station of transformational Pluto.

Archeology and Paleontology
- On December 23, 1938, during a station of Neptune, the coelacanth – a fish thought to have been extinct for millions of years – was caught by fishermen off the coast of South Africa.

- On September 19, 1991, the remarkably preserved body of "Otzi the iceman" was found high in the Alps, during a Uranus station in Capricorn (the zodiacal sign associated with mountains and hilltops).

- Several days later on September 22, with the station of Uranus still in effect (though with Neptune now grinding to a halt as well), the Huntington Library made the Dead Sea Scrolls available to the public for the first time.

- On July 17, 1959, archeologist Louis Leaky and his wife Mary discovered the first skull of Australopithecus in Tanzania, during a double station of Jupiter and Neptune in Scorpio.

- On November 4, 1922, Howard Carter discovered Tutankhamen's tomb in the Valley of the Kings, Egypt – an event widely regarded as among the greatest archeological discoveries in history. When Carter finally peered into the newly opened tomb, he was asked, "Can you see anything?" To which he replied, "Yes, wonderful things!" In addition to the full Moon in effect that day (with the Scorpio Sun also forming a trine to Pluto), Venus was turning retrograde that same day and forming a nearly exact sextile to Uranus. Venus rules beauty, of course, and retrogradation implies a backward-looking perspective, and both of those features were on display in the events of that day.

Media and the Arts

- Johnny Carson began his 30-year run as host of the *Tonight Show* on October 1, 1962, during a station of Saturn in media-oriented Aquarius; his term on the show ended on May 22, 1992, during another Saturn station in Aquarius.

- David Lean's film *Doctor Zhivago*, with its story centering around the Russian revolution, premiered on December 22, 1965, during a double station of revolutionary Uranus and Pluto.

- The Woodstock Festival ran from August 15 to 18, 1969, during a station of Saturn in Taurus. The Saturnian influence is visible in the dilapidated, mud-soaked conditions festival-goers contended with that weekend. (That same weekend also saw the most powerful tropical cyclonic system to reach landfall in recorded history, when Hurricane Camille hit the Mississippi coast, killing 248 people and causing billions of dollars in damage.)

- On February 3, 1959, a tragic plane crash took the lives of three prominent rock-and-roll musicians – Buddy Holly, Richie Valens, and J.P. "The Big Bopper" Richardson (an event memorialized in Don McLean's song "The Day the Music Died"). At the time, Neptune was virtually motionless, going retrograde just four days later on February 7.

- On June 11, 2015, Rupert Murdoch stepped down as CEO of 21st Century Fox – a move some commentators described as the "end of an era." That same day Mercury changed direction, and one day later Neptune went retrograde.

While one finds planetary stations involved with the careers of various musical groups, an unusual number of them seem to be constellated around the career of the Beatles. For starters, they began their 48-night residency in Hamburg, West Germany on August 20, 1960, on the same day Jupiter went direct in Sagittarius.

- The Beatles made their famous appearance on Ed Sullivan on February 9, 1964, during a station of Neptune.

- The Beatles' second movie *Help!* premiered on July 29 1965, the same day Neptune turned direct. (Note how Neptune's influence is visible even in the movie's title – a plea to be rescued!)

- From the moment of its release on June 1, 1967, the Beatles' album *Sergeant Pepper* was hailed as a milestone in pop music history. While the entire mid-Sixties reflected the influence of the revolutionary Uranus/Pluto conjunction in effect throughout that period, that dual-planetary influence was amplified dramatically in the days leading up to *Pepper's* release, with both Uranus and Pluto turning direct within less than 24 hours of each other.

- The Beatles' album *Magical Mystery Tour* was released in the UK on December 8, 1967, precisely as Saturn was stationing and sextiling Mercury and Mars, while inconjuncting Jupiter. Their much-criticized film of the same name premiered several weeks later on December 26, on BBC-TV, during a station of both Jupiter and Pluto (with Pluto turning retrograde literally within hours of the broadcast).

- The iconic cover for the Beatles' album *Abbey Road* was photographed on August 8, 1969, the same day Neptune turned direct in Scorpio.

Concluding Thoughts

I hope these examples have provided some sense of the potential influence of planetary stations on both the person and collective levels. The simplest point to bear in mind is that whenever a planet is relatively motionless, its energy becomes amplified, as are any aspects it may be making at the time. When studying the predictive trends in a horoscope – be it your own, a client's, or that of a nation—it's especially important to note those points when the activating planet changes directions, since those will serve as key trigger points. Planetary stations are just one tool in the astrologer's ever-expanding trade, but they can offer critical insights into our understanding of events in ways that may not be immediately obvious through other means.

Notes

1. My thanks to the late Goswami Kriyananda for suggesting the "branding iron" analogy regarding station points.

2. If you wish to study planetary stations in horoscopes but don't have a hardbound ephemeris on hand, there are several good ones available online for free. My personal favorites are those which feature color-coding to make the retrogradation periods more visible (like the one offered at Michael R. Meyer's helpful site www.khaldea.com/ephemcenter.shtml).

3. When studying a stationing planet in someone's chart it's also important to note whether it is the ruler of the Ascendant, Sun, or Moon sign, since that makes its impact more pronounced. For that matter, any house ruled by a stationing planet will assume greater importance in someone's life. Of course, it's also important to consider whether the stationing planet is retrograde or direct, since that will color its expression in other ways.

4. Besides his notoriety as an outspoken religious and political figure, Louis Farrakahn hails from an unusually diverse background that mirrors the Jupiter/Neptune conjunction trine the Sun in his natal chart. As a child, he was an expert violin player and had played with the Boston Civic Symphony by the age of 13, and in 1946 was one of the first black performers to appear (and win an award) on the *Ted Mack Original Ama-*

teur Hour. In the 1950s he began a professional music career recording several calypso albums under the name of "The Charmer," with one of his songs appearing on the top 100 Billboard chart for five years in a row.

5. Also, J.S. Bach composed what is arguably one of the most 'Plutonian' works in the annals of classical music – the famed *Tocatta* and *Fugue in D Minor*. Listen to any recording of this classic work and notice how its descending bass lines evoke the cavernous depths of the psyche in an almost *Phantom of the Opera*-like manner, while paradoxically hinting at the highest spiritual impulses as well.

6. Bill Wyman is a fascinating example of Pluto's influence in a number of ways. Besides providing the thumping bass lines for many of the Rolling Stones' greatest hits, Wyman has also enjoyed a hobby as an amateur archeologist, even designing and marketing a patented "Bill Wyman signature metal detector" that's been used to find ancient relics in the English countryside. Wyman also gained notoriety for his offstage bedroom exploits, admitting to affairs with nearly a thousand women over the course of his career.

16

Synchronicity and the Mind of God: Unlocking the Mystery of Carl Jung's "Meaningful Coincidence"

Those who believe that the world of being is governed by luck or chance and that it depends upon material causes are far removed from the divine and from the notion of the One.

Plotinus, *Ennead VI.9*

While preparing for his role in the 1939 film *The Wizard of Oz*, actor Frank Morgan decided against using the costume offered him by the studio for his role as the traveling salesman Professor Marvel, opting instead to select his own wardrobe for the part. Searching through the racks of second-hand clothes assembled over the years by the MGM wardrobe department, he finally settled on an old frock coat that eventually served as his costume during the movie's filming. Passing the time one day, Morgan idly turned out the inside of the coat's pocket only to discover the name "L. Frank Baum" sewn into the jacket's lining. As later investigation confirmed, the jacket had originally been designed for the creator of the Oz story, L. Frank Baum, and made its way through the years into the collection of clothing on the MGM backlot.

Most of us have, at some point or another, experienced certain unusual coincidences so startling they compel us to wonder about their possible significance or purpose. Do these strange occurrences hold some deeper meaning for our lives? Or are they simply chance events, explainable through ordinary laws of probability, as most scientists claim?

Among those who wrestled with these questions was the famed Swiss psychologist Carl Jung. Having experienced many such uncanny events himself, he coined the term *synchronicity* to describe the phenomenon of "meaningful coincidence." Whereas some coincidences were indeed without significance, he wrote, every so often there occurred confluences of circumstance so improbable they hinted at a deeper purpose or design in their unfolding.[1]

To explain such phenomena, he theorized the existence of a principle in nature very different from that normally described by conventional physics. Whereas most visible phenomena in the world seem to be related in a cause-and-effect manner, like billiard balls bouncing into one another, synchronistic events appear to be "acausally" related, as though linked by an underlying pattern rather than by direct, linear forces.

For instance, the presence of Baum's coat on the film wasn't caused by the making of the film, nor did the appearance of the coat somehow cause the making of the film; they simply were dual expressions of the same unfolding matrix of meaning. Jung went on to postulate two primary kinds of acausal relationships: between two or more outer events in one's life (as in the case of Frank Morgan), or between an outer event and an inner psychological state.

Since it was first published in 1952, Jung's concept has increasingly filtered into popular culture, having found its way into the plot lines of TV shows, works of pop-fiction like *The Celestine Prophecy*, and the lyrics of rock groups like The Police. In more scholarly quarters, there have been attempts to shed light on this theory through classifying various types of coincidence, scrutinizing it in terms of statistical studies, or even explaining it through quantum physics.

The search continues. In a letter to the late Victor Mansfield, Jungian disciple Marie-Louise von Franz wrote towards the end of her life:

> The work which has now to be done is to work out the concept of synchronicity. I don't know the people who will continue it. They must exist, but I don't know where they are.[2]

So what, ultimately, is the message of synchronicity, and how shall we best unlock its significance?

What I'd like to suggest here is the possibility that understanding synchronicity may require nothing less than a radically different cosmology than we're accustomed to, one with roots in a very ancient way of thinking – and one in which Jung's "meaningful coincidence" actually plays only a small part. Let me explain.

Most of us are familiar with the well-known parable of the blind men and the elephant. According to the story, a group of sightless men come across a great elephant, and each one tries to determine its nature from their own limited perspective. For the man grasping only its trunk, it seems to be a large snake, while for another, feeling only its leg, it's more like the trunk of a tree, and so on. Because of their partial and limited vantage points, none is able to grasp the true nature of the creature, since that can properly be understood only from a larger, more global perspective.

In much the same way, I'd suggest that by focusing our attention primarily on isolated coincidences we are only witnessing one small facet of a much larger reality, one with many different expressions and dimensions. Unlocking the true significance of Jung's theory thus requires that we step back and attempt to grasp the broader perspective of which synchronistic events are only a facet.

The Symbolist Worldview

What, then, is that "broader perspective"?

It's what I'll here call the *symbolist* worldview – a perennial perspective espoused through the centuries by such diverse figures as Plotinus, Pythagoras, Jacob Boehme, Ralph Waldo Emerson, and Cornelius Agrippa, to name just a few. For these and other figures, the world was viewed as infused with meaning, as "saying" something. As the Swedish scientist and mystic Emmanuel Swedenborg wrote in *Heaven and Hell*, "There is a correspondence of all things of heaven with all things of man."[3] The universe is a reflection of an underlying spiritual reality; all phenomena express the deeper ideas and principles of which they are a "signature," and can therefore be deciphered for their subtler significance.

For the symbolist, all events and phenomena are seen as elements of a supremely ordered whole. Like the intricately arranged threads of a great novel or myth, the elements of daily experience are viewed as intimately interrelated, with no event out of place, no situation accidental. Consequently even a seemingly trivial occurrence can serve as an important key toward unlocking a greater pattern of meaning: the passage of a bird through the sky, the appearance of lightning at a critical moment, or the overhearing of a chance remark – such events are deemed significant because they're perceived as interwoven within a greater tapestry of relationship.

Pervading the warp and weft of creation is a web of subtle connections sometimes known as *correspondences*. The American essayist Ralph

Waldo Emerson once said:

> Secret analogies tie together the remotest parts of Nature, as the
> atmosphere of a summer morning is filled with innumerable gos-
> samer threads running in every direction, revealed by the beams
> of the rising sun.[4]

Using more contemporary terms, these correspondences could well be
described as "acausal" connections, since they're not based on mechanistic forces of cause-and-effect, like our proverbial billiard balls on the pool
table, but on principles of analogy, metaphor, and symbolism.

For example, whereas scientists view the Moon as a material body
with certain measurable properties, such as size, mineral composition,
and orbital motion, among others, for the esotericist the Moon may also
be related to such things as water, women, the home, food, and emotions,
since these all linked through an underlying "lunar" archetype, or what
might be called the principle of *receptivity*. Understanding the language
of correspondences thus provides the esotericist with a skeleton key
toward unlocking the hidden connections which unite the outer and
inner worlds of our experience.

Since the advent of scientific rationality in the 17th and 18th centuries,
the concept of correspondences has been dismissed by scientists as nothing
more than an outmoded metaphysical fiction, comparable to a child's
belief in Santa Claus or the tooth fairy. Yet as soon becomes obvious to
anyone studying astrology for any length of time, such correspondences
are actually quite real and not merely the stuff of overactive imaginations.
Consequently, when the Moon is stressfully activated in a person's
horoscope, they may experience a rash of problems in their dealings
with women, say; or when Jupiter crosses over their Venus, they might
suddenly experience a run of good luck in matters involving romance
or money – and so on. Ultimately, the horoscope provides a complex
map of the symbolic correspondences that weave their way throughout
a person's life, in ways that are both testable and repeatable.

The Implications for Jung's Synchronicity

So how does the symbolist perspective force us to rethink Jung's synchronicity theory?

For one, in his formal writings on the subject Jung claimed that synchronicity was a "relatively rare" phenomenon.[5] But for the symbolist,

coincidence is just the tip of a far greater iceberg of meaning, the most visible feature of a pervasive framework of design and relationships that undergirds all experience. In a sense, the *entire world* is a vast matrix of "acausal connections" extending to every aspect of one's experience, from one's body and thoughts to every event and object in the environment. Said another way, everything is a "coincidence," insofar as everything *co-incides*!

Jung regarded the synchronistic event as an important "eruption of meaning" in our lives. But as divinatory systems like astrology demonstrate (and as I explore more fully in *The Waking Dream*[6]), there are actually *many* eruptions of meaning in our lives besides the occasional and remarkable coincidence, many of them equally important – marriages, births, deaths, graduations, job changes, chance encounters, accidents, nightly dreams, and many others. All these and more are "synchronistic" insofar as they correspond in acausal and meaningful ways to other unfolding patterns in one's life.[7] To borrow a phrase from William Irwin Thompson, we are like flies crawling across the ceiling of the Sistine Chapel, unaware of the complex archetypal drama spread out before us; what the infrequent and dramatic coincidence does is pull back the curtain for us on one small portion of that vast tableau of meaning.

For that reason, uncovering the truth of synchronicity won't be had through scientific methodologies or by carefully studying individual coincidences, but only through a broader philosophical inquiry into the symbolic nature of existence itself. As a result, unlocking Jung's "meaningful coincidence" may ultimately require a "unified field" theory of meaning that incorporates such diverse disciplines as sacred geometry, astrology, the theory of correspondences, chakric psychology, number theory, and a multi-leveled cosmology, to name just a few. Only within the broad framework offered by just such a Sacred Science can we hope to truly grasp the "whole elephant" of synchronicity, and not simply one of its appendages, as exemplified by the rare and dramatic coincidence.

And it's against this broader backdrop that we begin to glimpse some of the broader questions raised by synchronistic phenomena, such as: What could possibly organize the phenomena of our world in so profound and meaningful a way as this? In his book *A Sense of the Cosmos*, author Jacob Needleman offers a possible clue to that question with this comment about the uncanny symmetry displayed throughout nature's ecological web:

> Whenever we have looked to a part for the sake of understanding the whole, we have eventually found that the part is a living component of the whole. In a universe without a visible center, biology presents a reality *in which the existence of a center is everywhere implied.* (emphasis mine) [8]

Needleman's comments here could be read as a useful analogy for understanding synchronicity, too. In order for the diverse events of our lives to be interwoven as intricately and artfully as synchronicity implies, and as systems like astrology empirically demonstrate, there would seem to be a regulating intelligence underlying our world, a central principle that organizes all of its elements like notes in a grand symphony of meaning. One needn't think of this as involving a bearded, anthropomorphic deity on a heavenly throne somewhere, of course. As we saw at the opening of this article, the Neoplatonist writer Plotinus referred to this transcendent principle as simply "the One," while the Buddhists speak of "Big Mind," and the mystic geometers of old described a circle whose "center was everywhere but whose circumference was nowhere."

Whatever labels or terms one chooses, the phenomenon of synchronicity hints at a coordinating agency of unimaginable scope and subtlety whereby all the coincidences and correspondences of the world coalesce as if threads in a grand design, and within which our lives are holoscopically nested. Seen in this way, the synchronistic event can be seen as affording us a passing sideways glance, as if through a glass darkly, into the mind of God.

Notes

1. Jung, Carl. "Synchronicity: An Acausal Connecting Principle," in *The Structure and Dynamics of the Psyche, Vol. 8, Collected Works*. Princeton, NJ: Bollingen Series, Princeton University Press.

2. Quoted by Richard Tarnas, in *Cosmos and Psyche*. New York, Penquin Group, 2006, pp. 50-60.

3. Swedenborg, Emmanuel. *Heaven and Its Wonders and Hell*. New York: Swedenborg Foundation Incorporated, 1935.

4. Emerson, Ralph Waldo. *The Complete Writings, Vol. II*. New York: William H. Wise, 1929, p. 949.

5. The question as to the true frequency of synchronistic phenomena was a matter of debate even during Jung's lifetime, and at one point became a bone of contention between Jung and his colleague, the Swiss analyst C.A. Meier. Meier pointed out that if synchronicity is indeed a phenomenon at "right angles" to causality, as Jung claimed, then by definition it must manifest as commonly in our lives as does causality, not simply as an occasional feature. Conceding that point, Jung added a footnote in his book's second edition to that effect – failing, however, to credit Meier for clarifying that point for him. On being angrily confronted by Meier for this oversight, Jung modified the footnote (number 70) to include Meier's contribution, which in subsequent editions has read, "I must again stress the possibility that the relationship between body and soul may yet be understood as a synchronistic one. Should this conjecture ever be proved, my present view that synchronicity is a *relatively rare phenomenon* would have to be corrected." (Italics mine – R.G.)

6. Grasse, Ray. *The Waking Dream: Unlocking the Symbolic Language of Our Lives*. Wheaton, IL: Quest Books, 1996.

7. The frequency of synchronistic phenomena is just one of several ways the symbolist perspective forces a revision of Jung's theory, but there are others. For example, Jung regarded synchronicities as fundamentally *personal* phenomena, as arising out of the psycho-spiritual dynamics of a person's relationship with their world; yet the sheer pervasiveness of correspondences in our world, as demonstrated by astrology, for example, implies that synchronicity extends to the collective and universal levels as well. For example, one finds meaningful correspondences operating through history on a socio-cultural level as well, involving situations which extend far beyond the personal sphere – and indeed, the *universe itself* seems founded on the principle of correspondences, upon acausal connections of many types.

Also, Jung emphasized the element of *simultaneity* as a distinguishing feature of synchronistic events – i.e., coincidences occurring within the same moment in time, such as getting a phone call from an old friend just as you stumble across an old photo of them in your attic. Yet as both the symbolist perspective and Jung's predecessor in the study of coincidence, the Austrian biologist Paul Kammerer, argued, synchronistic phenomena can also involve *sequential* coincidences – e.g., such as coming across the same obscure literary reference several times over the course of a day. In short, synchronicity operates across all directions of time – forward, backward, and simultaneous.

Thirdly, Jung stated emphatically that synchronistic (and archetypal) events cannot be predicted beforehand. While that may be true in terms of their specific *forms*, astrology clearly shows it's possible to predict archetypal patterns of meaning in more general ways, far in advance of their happening. For example, we might look at someone's horoscope and see that Jupiter will soon be coming up to align with their Uranus, which strongly suggests they could experience lucky connections, coincidences, or opportunities at that point. While we can't say precisely how those events will manifest, the underlying archetypal energy itself is foreseeable.

8. Needleman, Jacob. *A Sense of the Cosmos: The Encounter of Modern Science and Ancient Truth.* E.P. Dutton & Co., Inc., 1975, p. 64.

Reprinted and revised from *The Quest* magazine, May/June 2006.

Conversations in Astrology

Interviews with Rick Tarnas
and
Laurence Hillman

Cosmos and Psyche:
An Interview with Richard Tarnas

In 1991, Richard Tarnas burst onto the literary scene with his book, *The Passion of the Western Mind*, an epic overview of Western thought from the ancient Greeks and Hebrews to the present. With sales of more than 200,000 copies, it drew praise from academic and literary quarters alike for both its insights and its eloquent style. Mythologist Joseph Campbell wrote that it was the "most lucid and concise presentation I have read, of the grand lines of what every student should know about the history of Western thought. The writing is elegant and carries the reader with the momentum of a novel … It is really a noble performance."

What virtually none of its readers back then could have realized was that Tarnas' book had originally been intended to be a multi-chapter historical and philosophical introduction to a far-reaching work on astrology. Books often have a mind of their own, however, and these chapters grew to be a full-sized independent work on the history of the Western world view, which Tarnas published separately as *The Passion of the Western Mind: Understanding the Ideas That Have Shaped Our World View*. As soon as he finished that task, he continued work on the astrological book, which was published as *Cosmos and Psyche: Intimations of a New World View.* The result of 30 years of research, it represents Tarnas' own unique contribution to the growing body of cutting-edge astrological evidence and philosophy. What made the release of this volume such an anticipated event in both the publishing and astrological communities was Tarnas' standing in mainstream academia. His first book, *Passion*, has become a standard text used in many universities in the United States and Europe, and Tarnas is often invited to speak at scholarly conferences around the world in fields other than astrology.

Tarnas was born in 1950 in Geneva, Switzerland and is a graduate of Harvard University and Saybrook Institute. For ten years (1974–84), he lived at Esalen Institute, where he was director of programs. Since 1993, he has been a Professor of Philosophy and Psychology at the California Institute of Integral Studies, often co-teaching with his colleague and long-time friend, Stanislav Grof. In 1995, Tarnas' short volume on the astrological Uranus, *Prometheus the Awakener*, was published by Spring Books, receiving glowing reviews from numerous astrological publications, including *The Mountain Astrologer*. I spoke to him just before the launch of *Cosmos and Psyche: Intimations of a New World View* in early 2005.

Ray Grasse: You once referred to your first book, *The Passion of the Western Mind*, as a "Trojan horse," in terms of laying the groundwork for your astrological writings for a general public. What exactly did you mean by that?

Richard Tarnas: In 1978–79, I wrote a monograph entitled *Prometheus the Awakener*, which by 1980 grew into a full book. But in the course of doing a final revision of the book for James Hillman's Jungian press, Spring Publications, I came to the decision that I should not publish it. That was because the book was directed too much toward only the astrological (and Jungian–transpersonal) community, and it focused too much on just one planet, Uranus. I felt that what I really needed to do was engage the whole planetary pantheon, all the planets, and write the book in such a way that it could serve as a bridge to the much larger world of intelligent readers who had not yet been initiated into astrology and who could not imagine taking astrology seriously.

Later, I did publish a shorter monograph version of *Prometheus the Awakener*. But as I took up the larger task of writing a book that could serve as a bridge to the non-astrological public, I started writing about the necessary concepts and the history of those concepts that I felt readers would require to grasp the evidence I would be presenting. I felt that people would need to understand the nature of archetypes, starting with Plato, and then how Aristotle's view shifted that understanding, and then the role of Christianity, and how the Copernican revolution shaped modern cosmology, and what depth psychology and Jung brought into the unfolding drama, and so forth. But as I started filling in the larger narrative to provide that kind of a history, it eventually turned into a book in itself, and that was *The Passion of the Western Mind*. In that book, I didn't explore or defend the astrological perspective; rather, I included it in the narrative, just as any good intellectual history of the West would discuss the role – the quite important role – that astrology has played in that history. But I did not examine the history from an explicitly astrological point of view in that book.

When *Passion* was published in 1991, it was taken up by many universities and colleges as a text. At this point it's used in – well, I stopped counting quite a while ago, after 80 or 90 colleges and universities were using it. And yet many professors and students who are using it would never guess that it was written by someone with an astrological perspective on all these developments. In a way I never expected when I was writing *Passion*, I ended up being invited to lecture at many universities and colleges, graduate schools and seminaries – sometimes even to give commencement addresses. So, in that sense, the book has become a kind of Trojan horse because it has been embraced by thousands of people who would not regard themselves as being the least bit open to astrology and its possible validity. But many of them have been writing me for years, asking when the next book is coming out. They're really interested. So when this comes out, at least to some extent there will be some surprises …

RG: Tell me, how did you get into astrology?

RT: It happened in stages, and then rather dramatically. When I was at Harvard, a Jungian analyst who was on the faculty of the Harvard Divinity School happened to be the therapist for my Radcliffe girlfriend; we became friends and met once a week for conversations about Jung and Freud and European ideas and culture. He had been trained by Jung and was Swiss by nationality. One week, he came in and must have asked me my birth data, because he started sharing with me something about my chart and where my planets were. I had no interest in what he was saying – this was just at such a different level of intellectual conversation than what we usually enjoyed, when we talked about what I regarded as more intellectually sophisticated and exciting topics. So, at that point, I steered the conversation as quickly as possible back to the usual channels of discussion. [laughs] After that, I had no significant exposure to astrology for several years.

My interest in astrology was really catalyzed during the years that I was studying and living at Esalen Institute in Big Sur, California. As I was working with Stan Grof there on my doctorate, we discovered, to our utter astonishment, that the most reliable indicator of the kinds of experiences that people would have when they were undergoing major psychological transformations or non-ordinary states of consciousness – whether through LSD therapy (Stan's specialization as a psychiatrist for 20 years) or other powerful forms of experiential psychotherapy – was transits to the natal chart. No other method of psychological testing, such as the MMPI or the Rorschach or TAT, had proved of any value for that purpose. So, that was what initially began my research, and after that it just grew. From early 1976, I started studying everyone who was at Esalen, both those who lived in the community and the people who were coming through for seminars. I did hundreds of analyses in the earlier years and then extended the scope of my research to famous individuals like Freud, Jung, Nietzsche, Virginia Woolf, Simone de Beauvoir, Newton, Galileo, and so on.

Finally, I expanded my research to include a systematic examination of correlations between the outer planetary cycles and major historical events and cultural trends, reflecting the archetypal dynamics of the collective psyche. To see how consistent those correlations were was probably the most astonishing – well, it's hard to say what was the most astonishing – but it radically extended the range of correlations for me and expanded the power of the astrological perspective and its implications. It wasn't just an individual phenomenon; it was an extraordinarily vast orchestration of cosmos and psyche, linking the planetary movements with the archetypal dynamics of the collective psyche. In the meantime, I became close friends with Charles Harvey, at that time the president of the British Astrological Association in England, and Rob Hand, both of whom visited me several times at Esalen. Their friendship and support of my work from the beginning was important for me, still in my twenties at that point. I only wish Charles were still alive today – he waited so long and patiently for this book.

RG: On the surface, your book appears to be especially concerned with that aspect of things, the astrological cycles of history. But on closer examination, it's clear there are actually several different concerns unfolding simultaneously. How would you summarize these?

RT: Well, the survey of historical correlations with the outer planetary cycles definitely constitutes the largest set of evidence that I present in this book, though I also discuss quite a few natal charts and personal transits. But the book is actually dealing with a number of things at once.

On one level, it's a sequel to *The Passion of the Western Mind*, so to a certain degree, it's extending that analysis by looking at how our modern understanding of the world was formed, how it developed. The new book looks at the crisis of the modern world view in our time, and how the disenchantment of the universe was connected with the forging of the modern self, so that the modern cosmos and the modern self actually arose together.

And a great price has been paid for the forging of the modern self. A kind of spiritual crisis has been produced by the disenchantment of the universe, and that spiritual crisis takes different forms. One of these is the sense of existentialist desolation we see underneath the surface of modern life, the result of living in a random, meaningless cosmos. Another is the fundamentalist religious antagonism to modern science and modern culture, the reactive rigidity that we see so strongly right now, the unwillingness to fully engage in the spiritual adventure of our time. Another enormous consequence of this disenchantment is at the ecological level, the global ecological crisis we see taking place, where the entire planetary biosphere can be viewed by corporations and policymakers as just an exploitable resource rather than something possessing spiritual value, something that has moral value, something to be regarded with a degree of reverence and respect, even religious awe.

So, the book explores how the development of the disenchanted world view and the crisis of the modern self are coming to a climax in our moment in history, and I discuss the possibility that the astrological evidence may have tremendous implications for that crisis of disenchantment. For one, it would suggest that the disenchantment of the universe is actually a temporary and local phenomenon. It's a paradigm that emerged at a certain time and place in history and has had a powerful grip on the modern mind, but it's not absolute. It's not the last word, science's final decision, the end of the story. The book sets out an analysis of the deeper metaphysical and cosmological drama of our time, and it seeks an understanding of our history that will make this crisis intelligible. I don't think this enormous historical development has simply been an accident: It's serving something larger in our collective evolution. So, the book is simultaneously a look at the metaphysical and cosmological drama of the current time, and it's also a look at our long, unfolding history and the evolution of human consciousness.

RG: You mentioned earlier about the book possibly serving as a "bridge" to the larger, non-astrological community.

RT: I think most astrology books are written for the astrological community, and are written with a framework of assumptions and a language that are familiar to the astrological community and to that community alone. What I tried to do was to write a book that I felt could serve as a bridge between the astrological community, on the one hand, and the larger general public of intelligent readers, on the other – those readers who have never encountered sufficient grounds for accepting the possibility that astrology has any value or validity.

One other major impulse informing this book is that, as the evidence unfolds and we explore different historical phenomena – like the revolutionary decades of the 1960s and the French Revolution during Uranus–Pluto alignments, or the great epochs of spiritual awakening and births of new religions that have coincided with Uranus–Neptune alignments, or the historical crises and contractions of the Saturn–Pluto cycle – the book serves as a kind of deep exploration of the human psyche itself. We see how everything, from scientific breakthroughs and cultural creativity to terrorism and apocalyptic beliefs, is shaped by powerful archetypal complexes, which have both positive and shadow sides that are enacted in history and individual lives. The existence of these archetypal complexes points toward larger spiritual dimensions of the human psyche and of collective human experience. So, in some ways, the book is also a psychological and spiritual exploration, as well as an historical analysis and a cosmological hypothesis. It's a work with several different levels of motivation going on at once.

In a sense, you could say I had four overlapping goals with the book: I wanted it to provide a helpful initiation, for as many people as possible, first, into astrology; second, into a spiritually informed world view and cosmology; third, into the archetypal dynamics of the collective and individual unconscious; and fourth, into a view of history as an evolution of consciousness that is itself an initiatory drama.

RG: In addition to its potential impact on our collective world view and on more practical matters like ecology, astrology also holds fairly profound implications for the individual, too, doesn't it?

RT: Yes. I think it provides the individual, first of all, with a new level of self-understanding, as it provides a new order of intelligibility for grasping the shape of one's life, the major themes of one's personality and psychological development. All sorts of diverse particulars in a person's life and character are suddenly revealed to have a coherent relationship to each other and to the cosmos. Things that may have seemed random or arbitrary are now seen to be part of a larger unifying pattern of meaning, which in turn is somehow grounded in the cosmos itself. The astrological perspective reconnects the individual to the cosmos. Many people who have entered deeply into astrology have the unmistakable sense that the cosmos is in some way meaningfully centered on the individual human being – and simultaneously centered on many individuals, on all individuals, on the Earth community. The individual person, as well as the Earth itself, is seen as a moving center of cosmic meaning in a much more mysterious universe than conventional modern science had assumed. So, one is freed from the typical alienated modern condition of being radically decentered in a random universe; instead, one feels that he or she is a genuine focus of unfolding cosmic purpose and meaning.

Such a perspective can be a great aid in psychological self-understanding. For example, we can recognize tendencies to project certain meanings onto situations or people, so we could be more on guard against those tendencies when they get in the way of living fully and authentically. Our capacity for critical self-reflection can be empowered in a new way, because we have more tools – we have the language of archetypal psychology, basically, but an archetypal psychology that has now been given a radically expanded context because of the archetypes' cosmic association with the planets.

What astrology does is to connect the findings of the depth psychological tradition all the way from Freud and Jung right up to archetypal psychology and transpersonal psychology – it takes that entire tradition of insight, which is really one of the great contributions of 20th-century culture, and connects it to the cosmos. The result is, you can both understand your own unique participatory inflection of these universal principles, and you can also get a sense for the timing of them – when a particular archetypal field will unfold in your life, the periods when they are more problematic and challenging – like an ongoing archetypal "weather report" on your life. It's a kind of surfing, in a sense – knowing your transits gives you a handle on how best to encounter the particular set of archetypal waves that are coming, how to ride them, when you would need to be cautious about something, when you would want to be aware of highly creative windows of time, and so forth.

RG: You saw the tragedy of 9/11 as serving as a benchmark of sorts in our collective attitude toward astrology, didn't you?

RT: Yes. That is something that a number of the advance readers of my new book have mentioned to me. Generally speaking, astrologers over the last several decades have become much more aware of the importance of the larger outer-planet cycles as they are correlated with the dynamics of the collective psyche, as they're evident in history. For example, when Saturn opposed Pluto in this most recent alignment of the Saturn–Pluto cycle, when it coincided with 9/11 and everything that happened afterward, there was a vivid awareness in the astrological community about the relevance of that planetary combination to the specifics of what was happening. This was different than in earlier years, when there was much more focus on the individual natal chart. Often it was just the personal horoscope, progressions, and transits that were attended to, with relatively little focus on the larger picture except in that subgenre of astrology called mundane astrology, which was not generally given the same attention as was natal astrology with its focus on the individual. I think this was part of the whole individualistic and humanistic culture of modernity with its overriding, and quite understandable, focus on the individual human being.

But what has happened in the last 15 or 20 years has been a gradually rising awareness of the relevance of the *zeitgeist*, the collective archetypal situation, and therefore the relevance of the outer planetary cycles. This reflects the deepening transpersonal awareness of our era. So, a number of my readers have mentioned how they were able to look at their own lives in terms of the major outer-planet cycles mentioned in this book, particularly those of the last half-century, such as in 1968–69 when there was a triple conjunction of Jupiter, Uranus, and Pluto; these readers could see correlations that were not as evident to them before, because they had been thinking more in terms of the individual chart and personal transits rather than the world transits relevant to the collective psyche.

RG: In the past, you've used a phrase that I think is useful for all astrologers to keep in mind when reading charts, or even looking at mundane (historical) patterns: "Astrology is archetypally predictive, not concretely predictive." What did you mean by that?

RT: I first used that phrase around 1980, when Rob Hand and I were attending an NCGR conference where a speaker got up and made a comment about how anybody who had planets at a certain degree of a certain sign was virtually certain to experience sexual assault or abuse of some sort in the course of their life. I was aghast at both the astrological misconception and the psychological harmfulness of such a statement. I watched a woman not far from me in the audience turn pale as she heard this. I was so offended by the speaker saying this and so concerned by the effect of her remark that, at the break, I went up to the woman in the audience and said that I believed that the speaker who made this statement was fundamentally misunderstanding how astrology works, because the nature of astrology is to be archetypally predictive, not concretely predictive. That is, when we know what a particular planetary alignment is, there is a wide range of ways in which that particular transit or natal aspect can manifest in our life and still be precisely reflecting the archetypal principles involved. But you cannot predict exactly which way it's going to come out in advance on purely astrological terms.

I believe that an understanding of astrology as archetypally rather than literally predictive is both more true to the reality of astrology and more empowering in its support of human autonomy. It supports the evolving capacity of the individual human being, with her free will and reflective consciousness, to bring forth the highest potential manifestation of a given archetypal complex, rather than simply be a puppet of it. The beauty of the astrological perspective and the gift it represents is that it provides us with a capacity to know what energies are constellated at a given time; this gives us a greater freedom to express these energies and embody them in a more intelligent and life-enhancing way, rather than just react or "act out" the archetypal complex in a predetermined or fatalistic way.

The deterministic view was more characteristic of earlier eras, though by no means was it universal even then. And to some extent, it still influences a certain number of astrologers today. Considerable harm is being done today by astrologers in counseling situations when they presume more knowledge than they have, and they issue definite, concrete predictions about what's going to happen, or what a person is going to be like, or what kind of relationship they will inevitably experience. Such predictions represent abuses of astrology, which can be quite destructive in their consequences. I strongly urge the astrological community to embrace an epistemological humility, to recognize that the limits of astrological prediction are closely intertwined with the greater richness of the archetypal understanding and the affirmation of human freedom. This issue underlies, at a deep level, one of the principal resistances that the modern mind has felt toward astrology – a healthy resistance, I might add. The modern mind (and the Christian mind before it) wanted to preserve human freedom, and astrology seemed to deny this.

It is possible to combine purely astrological cognition with some kind of clairvoyant or divinatory faculty to make a more concrete prediction. This was, I believe, more characteristic of earlier eras and of those astrologers in India (and a few in the West) who continue to practice in that manner. In the divinatory epistemology that Geoffrey Cornelius has explored, using horary astrology as a basic model, we have a helpful reflection on some aspects of this issue. But I believe that the practice of most astrologers today in the West, and the most influential texts of leading astrological authors, are better described in terms of archetypal understanding rather than literal prediction.

RG: One of the great delights of your book was coming across some of the fascinating synchronicities through history that I hadn't been aware of before, such as those centering around Herman Melville and his book, *Moby Dick*, or around the story of the mutiny on the Bounty.

RT: Yes. Well, let's take the latter as an example. One of the major patterns I've been examining over the last 30 years is the Jupiter–Uranus cycle. It's one that really stood out in the course of history in an almost brilliant way: Every time Jupiter and Uranus came into conjunction or opposition, there has been this extraordinary wave of cultural phenomena having a quality of either Promethean rebelliousness in society and politics or creative breakthrough in the sciences or the arts. It's astonishingly consistent, and I devote several chapters to that cycle in the book.

Many years ago, after studying the Jupiter–Uranus cycle as it manifested throughout the 19th and 20th centuries, I thought it would be really interesting to go back further and see what was going on in July of 1789, when the French Revolution began with the fall of the Bastille. Back then, in the 1970s, we didn't have personal computers or ephemerides that preceded 1800, so I had to wait each time for the mail to arrive with the charts I would order from Neil Michelsen for distant dates prior to the 19th century. When the chart for July 14, 1789 arrived, I discovered to my delight that there was in fact a Jupiter–Uranus conjunction within 2 degrees of exactitude. This aspect actually started late in 1788 and went through 1789, right up to September – the entire 14-month period that commenced the French Revolution.

I then noticed that in the spring of 1789, when Jupiter and Uranus were also closely conjunct, the mutiny on the Bounty took place, when Fletcher Christian and the mutineers rebelled against Captain William Bligh soon after they left Tahiti. As many people are aware, it's the most celebrated maritime rebellion in history. And the fact that this would have occurred precisely under the same Jupiter–Uranus alignment as the most celebrated political rebellion in history (namely, the Fall of the Bastille and the beginning of the French Revolution) seemed to me a marvelous synchronicity.

But apart from the astrological significance of this correlation, such a coincidence suggested something else: It pointed to the validity of Jung's basic conception of a "collective psyche," in which a particular archetypal complex can emerge in the collective psyche simultaneously in different places within the experience of different people, with no conventional causal connection between them. For example, there were plenty of rebellions happening throughout much of Europe right after the fall of the Bastille, under the Jupiter–Uranus conjunction, but these could be seen as having been at least indirectly set in motion by news of what had happened in Paris. But that's not what was happening in Tahiti in the South Pacific, since the Bounty had set sail from England in 1787. There was of course no way then that any communication could take place between England and the South Pacific. So, the evidence suggests that there can be the simultaneous emergence of a powerful archetypal complex in different places of the world, as if there were in fact something like a collective psyche.

RG: These correlations even continued unfolding afterward, didn't they?

RT: Yes. As the Jupiter–Uranus conjunction was happening, Uranus was also moving into a long-term opposition to Pluto, which occurred through most of the 1790s. This opposition between Uranus and Pluto, which might be thought of as the "Full Moon" version of what we had in the 1960s under Uranus conjunct Pluto, signaled a time of extraordinary revolutionary upheaval, sustained empowerment of the rebellious impulse toward freedom, artistic creativity and intellectual innovation, overthrowing constraints of all kinds, and so on. These things were happening right across the board in the 1790s as well as during the 1960s. And what's quite striking is that, following the mutiny on the Bounty situation, we saw this other side of the Uranus–Pluto archetypal complex emerge, where you have not just Pluto empowering and intensifying the rebellious, emancipatory impulse of Uranus, but you have it the other way around, with the Promethean impulse of Uranus liberating and activating the Plutonic forces of the libido and the id and the violent instincts. So, the period of the French Revolution witnessed a sustained eruption of violent impulses as well as an erotic emancipation very much like the sexual revolution and the violently rebellious era of the 1960s. But what happened with the mutineers after the mutiny is that Fletcher Christian and the mutineers went with a number of Tahitian women and men to another island, far away from Tahiti, called Pitcairn's Island; there, utterly isolated from the rest of the world during that entire Uranus–Pluto opposition in the 1790s, they went through a sustained period of intense conflict, violence, murder, jealousy, and power struggle, which was a microcosm of what was going on in Europe and in France, halfway across the world, under the exact same planetary alignment. The result was a kind of laboratory case of a continuing parallel synchronous emergence of the relevant archetypal complexes.

RG: In the last century, there have been some major revolutions in astrology due to developments like modern psychology and the advent of computers. Rather than ask you to try and predict what sorts of developments may lie ahead for astrology – that's a tough one when you consider that someone in 1850 could hardly have predicted either the advent of psychology or computers – I'll ask you this instead: What developments would you *like* to see take place in astrology over the next 50 to 100 years, to help take it to the next level, as it were?

RT: Well, I'd answer that on two different levels – one more practical and the other more philosophical.

On the more concrete level, there are a couple of very promising developments that have begun. During the Uranus–Neptune conjunction that occurred in the 1990s and that we're really just coming out of now, we've seen a rebirth of esotericism in many forms; among these can be included the movement of astrology into higher education and the universities. This has been happening both in England and the U.S. During the past decade, I've taught many graduate seminars in archetypal astrology for the California Institute of Integral Studies in San Francisco and at Pacifica Graduate Institute in Santa Barbara, both of which are accredited graduate schools. These courses, many of which I've co-taught with Stan Grof, have been extraordinarily popular with the students and have influenced the rest of their studies in psychology, philosophy, or cosmology. In the United Kingdom, Nick Campion and Patrick Curry have introduced astrology into the University of Wales, where they have accredited graduate master's and doctorate degree programs, just as we have at CIIS – in their case, with a focus on cultural astronomy and astrology. Liz Greene is now joining them there as well. And we have Kepler College here in the U.S.

This is the first time that astrology has been integrated into higher education and the university system since the end of the Renaissance and the early Enlightenment. That's an enormous development, and I believe it will happen more and more because, at its best, astrology represents an intellectually rich and rigorous mode of inquiry that can shine a light on many aspects of our history and culture. And the more that intelligent, educated people find this a central part of their educational experience – in many cases, one of the most exciting parts of their higher education – the more it's going to shift the cultural attitude toward astrology. It's not going to happen this year or next year, but I believe there will be a real shift within the next generation or so. Astrology's going to have a different cultural status than we are accustomed to now. Also, the work of Rob Hand, Robert Schmidt, and Robert Zoller over the same period represents another important development: recovering the classics of astrology and translating them from the various ancient languages into modern languages. This is a tremendous act of historical retrieval, not unlike what happened in the Italian Renaissance when the Humanist scholars were recovering Greek manuscripts and translating them into Latin and Italian and so forth – basically bringing them into the contemporary culture in such a way that it helped to catalyze the Renaissance itself. This is an enormous enrichment that began under this Uranus–Neptune conjunction and will undoubtedly continue.

RG: What would be the more philosophical level of what you'd hope to see ahead for astrology?

RT: Well, using what we already do see emerging, what I would hope to see would be a more profound grasp of the richness of the archetypal perspective in relation to astrology. The archetypal perspective in many ways empowers astrology to reach a depth of understanding that is not possible through mere "keywords," which has been the tendency in the past – you know, the 6th house rules work, health, servants, pets; Jupiter rules riches, travel, philosophy, priests, and so forth.

In turn, astrology can empower the archetypal perspective that has been developed in post-Jungian psychology, so this isn't just something you're trying to discern only through your dreams or your active imagination or analysis of contemporary films or whatever. These archetypal dynamics, your dreams, contemporary films, and the rest can all be illumined by knowing what planets are in alignment at what time, what kinds of geometrical alignments are being formed with respect to individual natal charts, and what similar archetypal phenomena have been observed with the same planetary aspects in other eras or other individuals.

I think the more that this power of the archetypal perspective (particularly, its multivalent and multidimensional nature) can be explored and developed within the astrological community, the more it will go a long way toward moving astrology out of the ghetto where it's been imprisoned. This ghetto of isolation and scorn has been created partly by the disenchanted modern cosmos and the skepticism of the modern mind, but to some extent it's also been a self-created ghetto, sustained by some of the basic intellectual presuppositions and methodological limitations of the way astrology has been practiced over the years. I believe that the development of an archetypal perspective could emancipate astrology from that self-enclosed ghetto so that it can begin to move into the center of culture, where it belongs.

Reprinted from *The Mountain Astrologer*, December 2005/January 2006.

All the World's a Stage:
An Interview with Laurence Hillman

I first met Laurence Hillman when we were paired up to share a hotel room at the "Cycles and Symbols Conference" in California in 1994. It was my first astrology convention – his, too, I learned. I'd been familiar with the work of his father, James Hillman, a well-known pioneer in the field of "archetypal psychology," so I was curious to not only compare notes as fellow astrologers but to see how that early psychological environment might have influenced his approach to the discipline.

What I encountered was not only a brilliant astrologer but someone with a keen psychological insight into the subtleties of the craft. Surprisingly, he mentioned that he'd never actually read any of his father's books from cover to cover (a way to differentiate his own developing ideas, I presumed); yet he went on to explain how growing up around psychologists – especially Jungians – caused him to be virtually "marinated in the archetypes" from an early age.

Since that first conference, he's gone on to give voice to that archetypal perspective in countless lectures and in two books: *Alignments: How to Live in Harmony with the Universe* (co-authored with Donna Spencer), and *Planets in Play: How to Re-Imagine Your Life through the Language of Astrology*. Raised in Switzerland and fluent in five languages, he moved to America at age 23 and has since lived with his wife and two daughters in St. Louis, Missouri. He currently maintains a busy astrological practice with clients around the world, and lectures frequently in both the United States and abroad. I spoke with him recently about the archetypal dimensions of astrology, the intermixture of astrology with theater, the Moon's Nodes, and his own perspective on current events.

Ray Grasse: Let's start at the beginning. How did you first get into astrology?

Laurence Hillman: Well, I was a bored teenager living in Zürich, Switzerland, and my mother was very interested in astrology. Just so I'd have something to do, she suggested that I study astrology with a family friend I'd known all my life, who was a professional astrologer. When I went to him, he said, "So, you're here to study astrology?" I said, "I guess." Then just ten minutes into my first lesson I had a clear vision that this is what I wanted to do for the rest of my life. My next thought after that was, I'm going to do this full-time when I turn forty, because there are a lot of other things I've got to do first. And that's pretty much what happened. I started full-time when I was 38, though by then I'd been practicing astrology for two decades already. So that's how it happened.

RG: You were raised in a heavily psychological household. I'm curious how that's affected your general perception of things, including astrology?

LH: Specifically, I grew up in an environment infused with ideas of depth psychology rather than, say, behavioral or motivational psychology. It was always natural to me to imagine us having a psyche, an often largely unconscious inner story. When I then learned about astrology I found it to be a perfect language to describe this psyche, what I experienced as a very active inner life. Later the use of theatre was very natural to describe what I imagined and experienced was going on inside of me and others. We have this inner stage, the psyche, where our play unfolds. The ten planets are characters interacting in our own drama. If we see the actors/planets as archetypal in addition to being personal, we can elegantly connect our own experiences to everyone else's. Studying that inner play – the "psyche-logia"–comes very naturally to me. Partly this is my nature, my inner play, but certainly it helped a lot to be raised in an environment where depth psychological language was prevalent.

There were other important influences as well. For instance, I went to a Rudolph Steiner school. These are called Waldorf schools here. Fairy tales, mythology, music and a largely right-brain education all contributed to encourage an imagination that was naturally there. Today the heavily Jungian slant in my early household still helps me to look at the world mostly through psychological lenses, and yes, that includes astrology. So I think about how and why people do what they do, but in a psychological way. I find myself constantly asking, "Hmm. What's the underlying story? I wonder what archetypal patterns are at work here?" I actually imagine a play going on in people, and in the heavens, at any moment. Our birth chart is a frozen minute in an ever-changing archetypal play.

RG: Perhaps we should clarify what "archetypal" means?

LH: The word means "first-molded" so the idea is that there is a pattern after which other things are shaped. Translated to human life archetypal patterns are experiences we all have, as though they were based on a prototype. For instance, the trickster is an archetype that appears in virtually every culture, in a myriad of forms. So we see that universality is one key to archetypes. In archetypal astrology the planets become archetypes. When we see Mercury in a chart we think of the trickster pattern. While we are observing a specific and personal expression of Mercury it is molded after some universal mercurial pattern that we all recognize. As an astrologer looking for other clues, for instance who is this Mercury character interacting with (the astrological aspects), I begin to understand how this particular Mercury is staging himself. Is he a fast-talking car salesman? Is he a magician, or is he a fool? Besides the most well-known archetypes such as the trickster, the hero and the teacher to name a few, I see more abstract concepts as archetypal as well. Take falling in love, for instance. If you fall in love in northern Siberia or southern Egypt, today, or 200 years ago, the human experience is remarkably similar. The longing for the beloved, the butterflies in the stomach, the sweet pain, these to me are archetypal because they are universal. We all experience and live these archetypes. Sometimes we enjoy them, other times we suffer them, and often we are not even aware of them.

RG: To your mind, what is the value of this archetypal way of understanding life?

LH: Well, the flip answer is that it's "preventive medicine." As I said to a client just this morning, I'd rather wonder and figure out what my Mars wants instead of being reminded of what Mars wants by a mugger! This is not about appeasing Mars, but about having an ability to choose how you want to experience Mars. You will experience Mars in your life. We all do, because Mars is an archetype. The notion that we have a choice in how we experience Mars seems counterintuitive to some of my clients because they have developed a notion that Mars is bad or harmful or dangerous. This is particularly true if any previous readings are based in Vedic astrological thinking. Here there is the idea of needing to appease a malefic planet. I do not subscribe to this idea at all for I do not believe in good and bad planets – or charts for that matter. Rather, I want to know the archetype that underlies Mars. I can get this by looking at a few key words for Mars – for instance drive, fight, separation, sexuality – and now I can begin to make a list of how I want to express that Mars and accordingly take action. What is psychological about this approach is that it denies a person the use of "blame psychology" as an excuse for their circumstances. We are not who we are because of what was done to us or because of our inability to change our chart. We are what we choose to do with all that we have experienced and how we step into our chart with that particular experience. We can take a seeming "problem" and once we understand the underlying archetype in that problem, we have enormous flexibility in dealing with it.

RG: Can you give a specific example of what you're talking about?

LH: Okay. Say I have a Moon square Saturn. The simplistic text-book interpretation might be that I had a cold mother, I tend to be depressed, inclined to melancholy, emotionally stunted, or some such thing. First off, I don't begin by looking at this Moon square Saturn as a problem. That is not my language though many astrologers – and clients with astrological experiences – would think of it that way. Instead I think of it as a story, and, like any good story there is a lesson to be learned here. If I consider learning to be valuable then there is gold in this lesson, in this story. I am fully aware that some lessons are difficult and some are downright awful. Of course I have seen all the simplistic text book manifestations I just listed. However, where does that leave my client? If I label this square a problem then I do more harm than help because I affirm what may be an awful list of experiences and feelings. I label it and bottle it and there is nowhere to go. So I take a different and practical approach, let me explain.

Imagine that the "Moon/Saturn problem" is over here in my left hand. I also ask my clients to hold out their left hand and visualize this. For whatever reasons, this square may indeed have manifested itself as one of the less desirable expressions I just mentioned. What is now in the left hand is the cumulative experience of a pained Moon/Saturn, a pile of old crap. So I ask my clients to hold out their right hand and we begin to look at what a Moon/Saturn story can also be, for instance – as an internalized example – holding one's feelings in check (quite useful for a judge or referee). An example of an externalized Moon/Saturn might be building houses for Haiti's earthquake survivors. These expressions of the "problem" are just as valid as the idea of the cold mother, my previous externalized example. What I'm saying is that if you understand the underlying pattern, you can now say "That old way is not how I want to live my Moon/Saturn. I want to live my Moon/Saturn by doing x, y, or z instead." And that new way is now over here in your right hand. There are as many ways to express or respond to the Moon/Saturn pattern as there are people in the world – and that's free will, that's choice. But if you simply look at what's in your left hand, you can spend your whole life in therapy, or analyzing, or blaming, or feeling guilty about what's going on over here in your left hand – or, you can say, "I acknowledge the pattern and honor the underlying archetypes by taking the following actions."

RG: This seems to bring us into the whole area of free will versus fate, doesn't it?

LH: There are lots of terms thrown around when it comes to fate, like karma, chance, luck, destiny, predestination, and others. Rather than try to understand what they all mean, let me explain what I understand to be happening in our lives. First we have a personality, and that's what is shown in the horoscope; it's the sum total of all these parts. Sometimes we call them character traits, sometimes we call them planets, sometimes we call them archetypes, but whatever we call them, they're basically the characters we get to know on our inner stage. Some are fighting, some are getting along, while some aren't relating to the others at all – and all that is shown in the chart. The chart reveals our general ways of relating to the circumstances that come at us throughout our lives. But the key is that there isn't just "one way" any one of those characters in you is going to express itself in the world, according to some sort of formula or the way it could ever be captured in a book. We need to add imagination back into astrology and make it less of a science and more of an art form. Nothing in the chart means anything in a certain way. Mars in the fifth house doesn't mean a person is going to be a gigolo, or feel especially libidinous. It could mean all of that but if we say "it is that" this then we are labeling and not allowing for an intuitive hit on how this particular

Mars is expressing himself in this particular person. This same Mars can also mean that they'll put a lot of energy into their kids, or their creative projects, and so forth. Mars is archetypally about drive, force, and feistiness, and wherever Mars is placed simply shows where you put that energy.

So "fate" is the fact that Mars needs to be expressed through the fifth house principle, in whatever sign it's in, and in whatever relationship it's in to the other characters on your inner stage. That Mars is not in the seventh, or the eleventh – it's relatively constrained, and that's your "fate." In turn, "free will" is the way you figure out how to express that Mars, how you respond to that energy. Your free will comes from the fact that there are as many ways to express that Mars as there are people on the planet. And there's no book or computer interpretation in the world that can possibly encompass all that. In *Planets in Play* I was asked by my editor to include chapters that list the planets in the houses and signs. The way I got around any sort of definition of what that "means" was by describing the clothing and the setting where a particular inner actor may appear. The idea was to stir the imagination instead of giving a recipe. For instance, for Mars in Cancer you will find, "This Mars is dressed in overalls. He is getting ready to paint the family room. You will find him constantly fixing and restoring heirlooms and other antiques that he chases after at yard sales…" and so on. This gives you an image. During a reading I can experience innumerable images for this Mars in Cancer emerging. I am bothered that some of my clients have come away from other astrologers where they were told absolutes, like "never," or "always" or "impossible." I don't see astrology in any absolutes and instead attempt to offer my clients imagery that they can then shape into something useful.

RG: A number of years ago I was surprised to hear you say you'd never actually looked at your children's horoscopes – not up to that point, anyway. I found that intriguing, because I couldn't recall any other astrologers who could say that.

LH: Well, I think having a child is like being handed a seed. And you plant it in the ground and you see what happens, and I'm more interested in finding out what kind of a plant it is than trying to analyze the plant before it's even sprouted. So I just thought it was more of a mystery, and more respectful to them, to "not know too much." It was a matter of honoring them enough to show themselves to me before I saw them in my own way, through a particular filter like astrology.

RG: So you wanted to experience their essence unmediated by an intellectual construct?

LH: Exactly. I also knew it was a fabulous tool and that I would use it if I needed to. And I have, and it's been very helpful.

RG: You were raised in Europe and only later moved to America, which obviously gives you a somewhat different perspective on our culture than most Americans have. The other day you mentioned about the ability of people to "start over" here and how it's different from what you saw in Europe. What did you mean?

LH: It's the whole "land of opportunity" idea. There are fewer second acts in Europe, but you really can start over again in America. There's a sense of renewal, a can-do spirit you hear so much about here. The employment rate here has changed quite a bit in recent years, obviously, but there still really are opportunities here. It's an attitude thing among the people: if you want to try something, Americans are generally going to say to you, go ahead and try it, good idea, go for it – that kind of a thing. Whereas in Europe they're going to tell you where you're going to fail. I realize that's a generalization, but it is the main reason why I live here. I also think this underlies the kind of astrology America has given birth to, the self-actualizing approach which views the horoscope not so much as a straightjacket but more as a springboard for one's potentials. When you look to the "old school" astrologers in Europe in past centuries, and even more so as you go East to India, it's more fatalistic, and also more cut-and-dried in terms of the various meanings for the planets and their placements. So I think that American attitude has affected even our astrology.

Of course it's been a risky progression in some ways, because that growing individualism can indeed become more narcissistic and greedy, it can become too self-centered. And part of growing up and becoming wiser for this country might be to reflect on things like, "What price did we pay for that narcissism in terms of slavery or no health care," for example, where you don't care about others so much because "self-actualization" is the main mantra. Social awareness is much greater in Europe, where you know you have a responsibility to your fellow man or woman beyond the conservative notion that it can all be done through charity.

RG: You've conducted workshops with figures like Laurence Olivier's son, Richard, and actor Mark Rylance, on the stage of Shakespeare's Globe Theater in London, where you've blended theater with astrology. What has been the purpose of bringing these disciplines together?

LH: Astrology is an extraordinarily complicated language. So over the decades I've been experimenting with various metaphors and visuals and have ended up with theatre imagery to introduce archetypal astrology to my clients in just a few minutes. I begin my readings with the image that the horoscope is a circular stage where the planets are acting out a play, and each one of them is an archetypal character. It's as though the heavenly bodies dropped onto that inner stage at the moment of one's birth and we took a snapshot of it from the rigging above, freezing that moment in time. The aspects tell us who is arguing with whom, who is kissing whom, and so forth. There's a story going on in every chart, just as there is in a real play. The planets are the "who," the aspects are the "what," the signs are the "how" and the houses are the "where." Of course the notion of blending astrology and theatre isn't new. There is a branch of astrology called experiential astrology and as the name says much of the powerful work done by those who have and continue to work in that way is about acting out. I use some of these techniques in workshops but blending astrology and theatre is an idea, a core metaphor that feeds my complete view of how archetypal astrology works. We already see hints of that merger between astrology and theater in ancient times and the application of these ideas became clear to me when I was invited to work on an archetypal approach to some of Shakespeare's plays.

When you read Shakespeare you soon notice that there are many astrological references in the plays beyond the obvious "star-cross'd Lovers." For instance there is that lovely line in *As You Like It* where Beatrice says: "A star danced and under that was I born" or in *All's Well That Ends Well* Helena says "...you must needs be born under Mars." The idea was that if a person is to fully appreciate Shakespeare a basic knowledge of astrological terms is necessary. Second, using an archetypal approach now, we asked questions such as what a "jupiterian" (speak: Jovial) Henry V might look like, versus a martial or saturnine one. This was especially fun when we worked with the actors in the group. This latter imagery also became the basis for my book *Planets in Play*, and I expanded on these ideas in a series of slide shows along with sound illustrating the primary astrological archetypes. I use these when I teach, and I've put them on my website as yet another way to help people see the archetypes in their lives. I love to create visuals as a stimulant for imagery, and it's actually one reason for why I went to architectural school. I have always had imagery and ideas in my head that I've wanted to share with others, and finding new ways to make things visible has continuously inspired me, I find it enriching. Unless you can see Venus in a chocolate mousse, I believe you are missing her full essence.

RG: You mention about there being hints of that merger between astrology and theater throughout antiquity, which is a fascinating subject in itself. Over the years scholars have talked about how the roots of modern theater can be traced back to the religious dramas and rituals of ancient times, going all the way back to the cave dwellers, possibly. But I think an argument could even be made that nearly all of the major religious rituals of history – be they Hindu, Egyptian, or Christian – were astrological rituals in a way, a kind of early "astro-drama," since they were acting out the seasonal or planetary energies of the time. Just look at Christmas, for example, and how it was associated with the Winter Solstice and the earlier celebrations of the Sun's return after the darkest point of the year.

LH: Celestial timing is something that's been a part of society for millennia, though we don't usually realize it. And I would add that in ancient times the only thing that was 100% predictable was the cyclical movement of the heavenly bodies, in particular, the Sun and the Moon. So all seasons, all order, all structure, all calendars, were indeed organized after that. There's nothing else we could be sure of. Hence all rituals, anniversaries, and celebrations were based on this certainty. That's what we knew, that's the "glue" that kept it together.

In an extraordinarily unpredictable world the sense that there was some kind of order was a huge factor. The only thing we could know for sure was that Mars was going to come back to that point in the sky, or that the days would start growing longer at a certain time of the year. In that way we organized time; the saturnine sense of structure came to us by following the planets. And all these rituals and celebrations were a way of organizing our world, as well as a way of aligning ourselves with those great cycles.

RG: Astrology also arose out of the sense that each of those cycles and celestial markers had its own unique meaning, with the rituals and celebrations being designed to honor, perhaps even exploit those distinct qualities.

LH: Right. This was all a way of bringing meaning to our lives, not only by organizing our world but by aligning our lives with the meanings of the cosmos. That's even acknowledged in a work like *Ecclesiastes*, in chapter 2 verse 3, where it talks about how there is a time for planting, a time for dancing, a time for loving, and so forth. Different times are better for some things than others. Response-ability means responding to what's happening. I think the ancients had a more subtle notion of time than we do. For instance, the Greeks distinguished between *chronos* and *kairos*. I would translate that into quantity of time and quality of time. The first of the two is easy because that is how we typically think: time measured in quantity. I have little time or much time. The notion of kairos is much more subtle. It implies that there are different kinds of time. Time has a particular quality. We still have remnants of that notion in our language when we say, for instance, "this is not a good time for me." That is an assessment of the quality of the moment that we are in. Astrology, in essence, is a tool to measure and describe the quality of time. The more we know about the quality of a moment the more we can decide what archetypes we wish to express then. Ancient celestial observers were keenly tuned into the qualities of the moments the planets marked off.

RG: Speaking of what's happening: as of this moment (June of 2010), we're in the midst of some powerful planetary patterns, especially the emerging t-square involving Uranus, Saturn, and Pluto. I'm curious to get your take on what's occurring on the global stage right now.

LH: The wonderful thing about mundane astrology (the branch of astrology that studies historical trends) is that it explains everything you see happening in the news. And that is extremely reassuring, because the one certain thing about transits is that they all have an expiration date, a shelf life, so to speak. That's a key idea, because it's saying that "this, too, shall pass." That transitoriness is a natural part of the cyclic nature of existence. (After all, we do call them "transits," don't we?!)

But as for the t-square, since Pluto is at the critical point of this current configuration, for me this period is really about the emergence of Pluto in some new way. It's a new awareness of what I call the "dark feminine." We are collectively horrified as Mother Earth in her magnificent force is bleeding and by that I mean we see devastating earthquakes, mining accidents and of course the Gulf oil spill. At some point even Mother Earth won't take it any more and Pluto is her messenger. I don't believe the Earth is coming to an end; that's a concept that's existed as long as human beings have been around; it's the fantasy of end times. But there's constantly this reminder that we've got to do something about how we're using the resources that come from Mother Nature. This is about embracing that dark feminine, the yin in the world.

What Pluto's asking everybody is, where is your deepest "hole"? And what are you trying to fill it with? You know, we're going to that level of depth where people have to understand their deepest psychological fears. For example, if they're getting plastic surgery, maybe it's their fear of death. What are you really trying to fill? If you're consuming stuff, if you're filling yourself with busyness, with cell phones, text messaging, and so on, what are you really afraid might happen in the stillness that Pluto offers?

And it's this slow emergence of a realization that the pillars of our old ways – such as science, religion, justice and even capitalism – are no longer working. We are finding out that these pillars were not made of stone but of wood. Science can't fix the leak in the Gulf, religion doesn't have answers for an increasing number of people, "justice for all" seems increasingly distant, and capitalism itself isn't looking so rosy at this point. Pluto to me feels a lot like termites eating away at these wooden columns of our temple. It's very slow and scary, you don't realize how much has crumpled until the roof is practically on top of your head. These times are challenging, of course, and they also offer a challenge.

RG: The subject of your first and co-authored book was the *Nodes of the Moon*. If the horoscope reveals the different characters on one's inner stage, where does the North Node fit into that picture?

LH: First, I define the personality as the way we express our psyche. Simply put, who we are as the sum total of all these inner parts. Besides the personality, and separate from it, there is this part of us that I call the soul. The soul uses the personality and the person to experience certain things in this life. The soul is immortal and travels through many lives. I've used the imagery of an endless train track to illustrate the path of the soul through many lives. It comes from somewhere and goes somewhere. We then imagine that we are born at a specific place along that track. This is the South Node, where the soul enters the body. It's where you've come from; it's where you already have a bunch of Ph.D.'s under your belt. So it's a comfort zone where you like to hang out, simply because you know it.

But the North Node is where that train track is heading, it's a point of new learning. The house position is actually much more important than the sign, because the house tells you where, and the signs have to do with how. For me, the North Node is an area of your life that you came here to get to know better. The concept is as simple as that and also as complicated and rich as that. It's about getting to know life better.

RG: To "know life better"– towards what end, specifically?

LH: Several things. I find that no matter how much we try to avoid our calling – this exploration of the house indicated by our North Node in the context of our whole chart – we end up hearkening to the call at crucial moments. The rewards, and what I mean with "getting to know life better," is that we feel emotionally fulfilled, mentally focused, and spiritually aligned. For lack of a better term, a sense of happiness. But in a larger sense the Nodes relate to the notion of reincarnation and how there is this sense of direction we are heading in. There is actually a direction on the soul level, which is not personality-based but soul-based. Particularly when we're lost, the solutions never really come from the personality level, because the ego personality doesn't see the big picture. Of course, people always try to solve it from the level of the personality – that's what we do in therapy, that's what we do in every self-exploratory type of process. But the gift of astrology is it can take you outside of the personality, outside of personal history, outside even of the chart to this more esoteric spiritual direction. Follow the Yellow North Node! (Laughs.)

Here's an example from *Alignments*: Charlie, a middle–aged manager came to see me many years ago because he "wanted to change things a bit." His North Node is in the fifth house. Before he arrived I was wondering how he may be expressing his creative side. His North Node was also in Taurus and I had thought to myself that perhaps his creative pursuits were practical and even artistic. Charlie arrived looking extremely sad and gave me much more information than I asked for. He complained about his seemingly endless responsibilities: his co-workers, his demanding wife, his kids in college, you get the idea. I asked him, "Charlie, if you had no responsibilities and could do whatever you wanted, what would you do?" He looked at he floor, sobbing bitterly now, and said quietly, "I would sculpt." The place that Charlie felt comfortable and spent most of his time in was his eleventh house. The corporation, the group, the Big Idea and helping others do well. He wasn't paying enough attention to his soul's compass and this was enormously painful.

RG: The notion of the "soul's compass"– that's interesting.

LH: To me, the North Node is the description of a place that you came here to explore. It's not a job description, it's not a lesson plan, it's the description of a place. If for instance you learn that your calling in life is to go to Paris, you can say, "No, I don't like the French and I'm not going there"– or, you can spend your whole life learning the language, falling in love in the Spring, going to every museum you can find, eating all the food you can afford in Paris, and that would be a different way. And the key is, Paris doesn't care, because Paris is just a place. So the calling has no vested energy, it is simply a place that sits there, and your job in life on a soul level is to go and explore that. This example shows you how the calling differs from the archetypes on your stage. You can't ignore your inner characters but I have seen many people in my practice who have become completely disconnected from their calling.

Now, there are two things about the calling that are crucial. The first is that nobody wants to do it! I have yet to meet somebody who gladly tiptoes through the tulips to their calling. (This is presuming there are no planets sitting on that axis, which changes things considerably.) So the first thing is that nobody really wants to do it. They may long to – that's different. But they'll usually fall back on their comfort zone, as indicated by the South Node and the house it's in, simply because that's what they already know.

The second point that I've learned about the North Node is that exploring it is a lifelong process. So the day you can say, "I truly and fully understand Paris," to go back to my earlier example, that's the day you can close your eyes and stop breathing, because you're done for this lifetime. The fact that you're alive means you're not there yet. The exploration of your North Node is not something you do when you're nineteen, get a certificate for, and then you're done with it. It is a lifelong task.

Reprinted from *The Mountain Astrologer*, February/March 2011.

Other Titles from The Wessex Astrologer
www.wessexastrologer.com

Martin Davis	Astrolocality Astrology From Here to There	Joseph Crane	Astrological Roots: The Hellenistic Legacy Between Fortune and Providence
Wanda Sellar	The Consultation Chart An Introduction to Medical Astrology Decumbiture	Komilla Sutton	The Essentials of Vedic Astrology The Lunar Nodes Personal Panchanga The Nakshatras
Geoffrey Cornelius	The Moment of Astrology		
Darrelyn Gunzburg	Life After Grief AstroGraphology: The Hidden Link between your Horoscope and your Handwriting	Anthony Louis	The Art of Forecasting using Solar Returns
		Lorna Green	Your Horoscope in Your Hands
Paul F. Newman	Declination: The Steps of the Sun Luna: The Book of the Moon	Martin Gansten	Primary Directions
		Reina James	All the Sun Goes Round
Jamie Macphail	Astrology and the Causes of War	Oscar Hofman	Classical Medical Astrology
Deborah Houlding	The Houses: Temples of the Sky	Bernadette Brady	Astrology, A Place in Chaos Star and Planet Combinations
Dorian Geiseler Greenbaum	Temperament: Astrology's Forgotten Key	Richard Idemon	The Magic Thread Through the Looking Glass
Howard Sasportas	The Gods of Change		
Patricia L. Walsh	Understanding Karmic Complexes	Nick Campion	The Book of World Horoscopes
M. Kelly Hunter	Living Lilith	Judy Hall	Patterns of the Past Karmic Connections Good Vibrations The Soulmate Myth The Book of Why Book of Psychic Development
Barbara Dunn	Horary Astrology Re-Examined		
Deva Green	Evolutionary Astrology		
Jeff Green	Pluto 1 Pluto 2 Essays on Evolutionary Astrology (edited by Deva Green)		
		John Gadbury	The Nativity of the Late King Charles
Dolores Ashcroft-Nowicki and Stephanie V. Norris	The Door Unlocked: An Astrological Insight into Initiation	Neil D. Paris	Surfing your Solar Cycles
		Michele Finey	The Sacred Dance of Venus and Mars
Martha Betz	The Betz Placidus Table of Houses	David Hamblin	The Spirit of Numbers
Greg Bogart	Astrology and Meditation	Dennis Elwell	Cosmic Loom
Kim Farnell	Flirting with the Zodiac	Gillian Helfgott	The Insightful Turtle
Henry Seltzer	The Tenth Planet	Christina Rose	The Tapestry of Planetary Phases

Lightning Source UK Ltd.
Milton Keynes UK
UKHW021930250619
345010UK00005B/108/P